OVERCOMING
AVERAGE

TABLE OF CONTENTS

DEDICATION

March 14, 1994, will go down as the second greatest day of my life. This was the day that I first met my wife Sandy. At that time she was Sandy Heidenreich, but eight months later she became my wife.

I lovingly dedicate this book to my dear wife because without her I would have never overcome many of the obstacles and battles that we've faced. Throughout the years I have watched many men, more talented and gifted than myself, quit the ministry because their wives wouldn't let them continue.

This has not been the case with my wife. Throughout the years she has been my biggest cheerleader and defender. She has encouraged me when others have attacked. She has given spiritual advice when the doors of Heaven seemed to be closed. She has been the rock of Gibraltar as we've faced trials and hardships. Without her I would have never been able to accomplish the overwhelming achievements that God has allowed us to conquer together.

My wife Sandy has been everything a wife should be. When we got married, the only thing we had for a house was a GMC pickup truck with a camper shell on the back. Within two years we graduated into a fifth-wheel trailer, but even that wasn't everything some would think it to be. She graciously helped me empty the holding tanks, thaw out the pipes in the middle of winter and stand on the side of the road for hours as we waited in the mountains of Colorado for a tow truck to tow us to the nearest mechanic. She has never complained about not having enough finances, but instead she has helped pinch pennies when money was tight.

Furthermore, I have watched my dear wife put up with my busy travel schedule for over two decades, and not one time have I heard a complaint. When other preacher's wives have griped and complained about their husbands always being gone, I have watched my wife graciously accept God's plan for our lives. With a good spirit she has accepted the role of her husband being gone for two-thirds of every year.

Proverbs 31:8 says, *"Her children arise up, and call her blessed; her husband also, and he praiseth her."* My wife certainly deserves every bit of praise that comes her way. She has quietly stood in the shadows and not demanded attention, but helped her husband overachieve in many areas of his life. She is in every sense of the words, a help meet. My ministry would not be what it is today if it were not for Sandy Domelle.

Of all the people who deserve to have a book like this dedicated to them, my wife, Sandy, deserves that honor. She is the love of my life, and without her I would not have overcome the obstacles of life that have come my way. She has in every way helped me travel the road to overcoming average.

FOREWORD

Overcoming Average – what an incredible book! Having read through it, I can attest that you will not only enjoy the content therein, but also be motivated and helped by the author's expertise on this subject. This book is a must for young people as well as for adults and should be a ready source in the Christian home.

When I was a boy, my father collected good Christian records for our family. He also accumulated a small library of books that we children could pore over in a designated area of our house. *Overcoming Average* is most assuredly one of those books that young people of every generation should read and whose principles should be applied to daily living. I trust that, as you read through this book, the words will inspire you to be used of God regardless of what we may consider merely *"average"* abilities.

I have known Allen Domelle since he was a young boy, and I have watched him grow up to be a faithful servant of our Lord. I know you will appreciate him as I do. May God use this book to help each of us become all we can be for the Lord.

Dr. Jack Trieber
North Valley Baptist Church
Santa Clara, California

1

You Will Never Make It

"My advice to you is don't go into evangelism. You will never make it." This was the advice a preacher gave me when I asked his counsel concerning going into full-time evangelism. I do not know what his reason was for giving me that advice. I do know one thing; in his opinion I would never make it as an evangelist. There was no pat on the back. There were no words of encouragement. The only thing I understood from his advice was that I was too average to make it as an evangelist.

To be honest with you, I am an average person. I was not reared in a wealthy home. I did not have famous parents. I am a person of average intelligence. In fact, if you were to compare yourself to me, you would probably find that there are many similarities.

I was born into a preacher's home in Chattanooga, Tennessee. My father was attending his last year of Bible college when I was born. From the time my parents left Bible college to the time I left home for college, I lived in seven different states and nine different cities. When I talk about how much I moved during my childhood, many ask me if my parents were in the military. Though I don't remember much about some of the places we lived, I do know that each place had an impact on instilling in this average boy the importance of overcoming average.

When I was 13 years of age, I was called to preach. Every year in our church we had a missions conference, and that year was no different. Bro. James Holder was preaching that night, and he preached about Jonah running from God. I was not running from God, in fact, I was involved in my home church. But, that night God did something special in my heart. I became burdened for my country. As I heard Bro. Holder talk about Nineveh headed for destruction, I knew someone needed to do something for America. That night when the invitation was given, I walked the aisle and surrendered my life to be a preacher of the Gospel. At the altar that night I told God, "God, if you can use someone like me, then I will give the remainder of my life to serve you."

When I was 15 years of age, the people who directed our junior church were relocated to another place by the military. That left a gap open in our church, and it seemed as if there was no one who could preach in the junior church. I went to my father and asked him if he would allow me to fill in until he could get someone else to take over the junior church. I was a fill-in until the day I graduated from high school.

I left for Bible college with high hopes that God could use me. I knew I was not a great preacher, and I knew that God had His work cut out to use this average boy; but, I had a belief inside that God could use me. That year while I was at college, God showed me that He wanted me to be an evangelist. I didn't know how to do it, but I knew that God wanted me to be one. When I left college, one of the college professors pulled me aside and told me that God would never use me. That was quite a blow, but I didn't let that stop me from doing what God called me to do.

When I got back home, I picked up the duties I previously did with the intention of eventually going into full-time evangelism. I remember the night that God made it very clear that I needed to quit my job and go into full-time evangelism. The only problem was that I only had four meetings booked, and I needed God to come through.

Because this was such a big step of faith, I asked my father if he would allow me to get some counsel from a preacher in northern California who was very well-known at the time. (Let me say that this preacher is no longer there.) The preacher asked me what he could help me with, and I told him about God's call on my life. I told him I wanted to get advice from him that would help me fulfill God's calling. After talking for fifteen minutes or so, that preacher told me that I would never make it in evangelism. He told me that nobody knew me, my father or the church I attended.

He told me that if I did make it that I would never preach in a church of over one hundred. He continued to say that he would never have me preach in his church. His last piece of advice was to give up the dream of being an evangelist and go back to my home church and simply stay involved in my church.

What the intent of that preacher was I do not know. One thing I do know is that I walked out of his office with a great determination to prove him wrong. I reminded myself that man did not call me, God did, and if God called me then He could use me. On top of that preacher's admonition, many of the established evangelist of that time also wanted nothing to do with me. They never lent their advice or help to this young evangelist. All I had was God and His calling.

Certainly, nobody would have ever called me the next Billy Sunday or Jack Hyles. Most who could have helped me make it in evangelism wanted nothing to do with me. Most looked at me as an average person who would probably never make it in this difficult field.

I'm certainly not the next Billy Sunday, but I can say that for over two decades God has used this average preacher to become an overachiever in the eyes of those who said he would never make it. I may never preach the city-wide campaigns that Billy Sunday and John R. Rice preached, but I know that God has allowed this average preacher to overcome average by seeing thousands of people saved and several hundred young people being called into the ministry. Many of those young men have gone on to become pastors, evangelists and missionaries around the world. God has used this average preacher to write several books, send out thousands of devotionals worldwide on a daily basis, and establish the *Old Paths Journal*, which is an online paper that is read in over ninety countries.

2 Chronicles 16:9 says, *"For the eyes of the Lord run to and fro throughout the whole earth, to shew himself strong in the behalf of them whose heart is perfect toward him..."* I determined many years ago that if I made it, then God would have to show Himself strong through my life. Early on in my ministry I claimed Psalm 81:10 that says, *"I am the Lord thy God, which brought thee out of the land of Egypt: open thy mouth wide, and I will fill it."* I simply opened my average spiritual mouth wide for God to use, and He has taken this average person and helped him to overcome what others call average.

The purpose of this chapter is simply to show you that you don't have to be considered the most likely to succeed to overcome average. Just like myself, you may be an average person who many don't believe will ever become something, but I want to encourage you that if God can take this average person and help him overcome average, then he can take you and help you overcome average. Don't listen to the naysayers who tell you that you can't do it. Find your motivation to overcome average from God's Word and His will. I consider myself an average person, but I didn't want to stay average. Despite other's lack of belief in what God could do through me, I decided to open my mouth wide and let God fill it, and He has! With God's help I have overcome what others called average. I believe you too can overcome average if you will open your mouth wide and believe that God can do something through you. The pages of this book have been written to show you how God can use you to overcome average.

2

More Than Conquerors

Most people are not a Bill Gates or a Steve Jobs. Most people will not be a Hank Aaron or a Johnny Unitas. Most people will never be a Charles Spurgeon, J. Frank Norris, Jack Hyles or Lee Roberson. Most people will never be a George Washington or a Ronald Reagan. We look at these people who were definitely above average, but let's face it, most of us are average people with average talent.

When we look at names like those above, we see their talent and say, "I could never do that." We look at their achievements and many times think these people must have been talented or gifted individuals, and in some cases they were, but most of these men were average men who decided to be more than conquerors. They decided to take the talent they had and build upon it. They were not satisfied with just being average, but something inside of them drove them to do more than the average. This is why they became known. History is filled with people who many would consider overachievers.

Benjamin Franklin is one of history's greatest overachievers. Franklin was one of seventeen children. Many would consider Franklin a brilliant mind, but what most don't realize is that he only had two years of formal schooling. He made up for his lack of schooling by reading many books and gaining knowledge from others. Though he was considered academically below average, he overcame average through hard work, ambition and thrift. At the end of his life he was known as a scientist who contributed much to the nature of electricity. He served his country, state, and city as a councilman, postmaster, recruiter of the Pennsylvania militia, Speaker of the Pennsylvania State House, delegate to the Second Continental Congress, ambassador to France, President of Pennsylvania, and Founding Father. His writings are still referred to today by many politicians, educators and motivational speakers. This is not bad for a man who only had two years of formal schooling. He certainly conquered his weaknesses and overcame average.

Another famous overachiever was Ray Kroc. Kroc was a high school dropout, who, with a little dishonesty, got into the military as an ambulance driver in World War I. The war ended before he had a chance to see action. After trying a few different ways to make a living, he soon found a small niche in selling milkshakes. For seventeen years he traveled the country selling his milkshakes until he became intrigued with a hamburger restaurant. With a vision for this restaurant to become a national food empire, he purchased this small restaurant at 53 years of age.

This small franchise is today the largest burger franchise in the world known as McDonald's. What most don't know is that Mr. Kroc suffered from diabetes and arthritis. This high school dropout is still influencing the food market. Though most would have considered him an underachiever when he dropped out of high school, he did not allow other's opinions of him to stifle his dream. Instead, he overcame average and went on to build the largest burger franchise in the world.

Pages could be filled with those who've overcome average throughout history. There was Thomas Edison who was kicked out of school and only had three months of formal schooling, was partially deaf, and failed over a thousand times to make a light bulb, but today is known as one of the greatest inventors of all time. We could talk about others who overcame average like Abraham Lincoln, Sam Walton, Clarence Thomas, Booker T. Washington, and Isaac Newton. All of these average people, and many more, became overachievers. Each one of these people were considered average or below average, but they did not let the perception of others stop them from overcoming average.

The Scriptures are filled with people who overcame average. One of the greatest overachievers in the Scriptures is Gideon. Gideon was an illegitimate child. His step brothers did not like him, and he was certainly not considered one who would achieve greatness. Yet, God believed that Gideon could do great things when He said in Judges 6:12, *"And the angel of the LORD appeared unto him, and said unto him, The LORD is with thee, thou mighty man of valour."* Gideon wasn't sure that God knew what He was talking about, so he put out a fleece and God showed him that he was to lead Israel out of bondage. Gideon took three hundred men and defeated a professional army that no other country could defeat. Gideon certainly overcame average.

I think of David, who is known as one of the greatest kings of all time. Yet, when it came to his childhood, his own dad and preacher didn't believe that God could make a king out of him. When Samuel came to anoint one of the sons of Jesse to be king, Jesse brought all of his sons before Samuel but one, David. David was never notified that Samuel was coming to anoint one of them to become king of Israel. Instead, they left him in the field because his father did not think he could do it. Finally, when David was brought before Samuel, God rebuked Samuel in 1 Samuel 16:7 when He says, *"But the LORD said unto Samuel, Look not on his countenance, or on the height of his stature; because I have refused him: for the LORD seeth not as man seeth; for man looketh on the outward appearance, but the LORD looketh on the heart."* Though nobody else believed in David, he had a God Who believed in him, and they two accomplished great things together. There is no doubt that David overachieved.

The Scriptures are filled with people who overcame average. There was Abram, Rahab, Joshua, Moses, Shadrach, Meshach, Abednego, Peter, Paul, John the Baptist, the boy with his lunch and the maid who notified Naaman how to have his leprosy healed are just a few who could be discussed. Many of these were just like you. They didn't have much talent and they weren't considered people who were the most likely to succeed. Yet, they conquered whatever weaknesses they had and overcame average.

The verse I have signed in Bibles throughout the years is Romans 8:37. This verse says, *"Nay, in all these things we are more than conquerors through him that loved us."* I took this as my life verse because I knew I was not the most talented of individuals, but I had a God Whom I knew could do great things through me.

You will notice this verse says, *"more than conquerors."* God wanted us to know that we could do more than those who have conquered great things. These names in history are certainly great names, but through Christ you can do more than they. God promised that with His help we are more than conquerors. Yes, there are those who have conquered great feats in history, but with God's help you can overcome average and do more than they. That means you can do more than a Bill Gates, Thomas Edison, Benjamin Franklin and others. This verse shows us four things we must understand if we are going to be more than conquerors.

1. Inside of every person is the capacity to overcome average.

When God says that we are *"more than conquerors,"* He is saying inside of every person there is the capability to do more than what others think you can do. You can sit and think you will never be able to do what others have done, or you can take God at His Word and realize you can overcome average. It doesn't matter what your background is, your education level, how well people know you, the side of town in which you lived or the amount of money you have in your checking account. You can overcome average if you will simply believe God when He says that we are *"more than conquerors."*

2. You must not let the perception of others defeat you.

One of the greatest things that any overachiever has to quickly overcome is other's perceptions of them. You will never overcome average if you let other's opinions of you cause you to live a life of defeat. God says that we are *"more than conquerors."* So, who are you going to believe, the people who have no idea about your future, or the God Who created you for a specific purpose?

If I had let the preacher's advice stop me from becoming an evangelist, then I would have never accomplished all that God has done through me.

God can only help you overcome average if you will act upon that which you know God wants you to do. Overachievers acquire a deaf ear to the naysayers. Trust me, there will always be naysayers in life. Just because someone says something about you does not mean you have to live down to their little vision. You must trust God's vision and realize that we are *"more than conquerors."*

3. You must have a drive to conquer that which attempts to limit you.

If there is anything you can learn from history's overachievers, it is that you must have a drive to conquer your limitations. There is no doubt that you know your weaknesses. You daily stare your weaknesses in the face. Those weaknesses can either be the catalyst to inspire you to overcome average, or they can be the obstacles that stop you and cause you to be content with being average.

Inside of every person who has overcome average is the drive to prove the naysayers wrong. If you are waiting for others to tell you that you can overachieve, then you will never overcome average. You must claim 1 John 4:4 that says, *"Ye are of God, little children, and have overcome them: because greater is he that is in you, than he that is in the world."* Let God's belief in you be the driving factor to help you conquer every obstacle that tries to keep you from being *"more than conquerors."*

4. You are the only one who ultimately limits your potential.

Ultimately, it comes down to you. Romans 14:12 says, *"So then every one of us shall give account of himself to God."* It really doesn't matter what others have said about you, it all comes down to what you are going to do. Are you going to let the negativity and lack of vision that others have stifle your future, or are you going to let God work through you and become *"more than conquerors"*? It is up to you! Those who overcome average look the obstacles of life in the face and decide to make them opportunities to show that it can be done. Every person who has inspired you did so because of something they overcame. You can be that inspiration to others if you will decide to become *"more than conquerors."*

Before you go on to the next chapter, it is time you face your limitations. It's time you look at them and tell them that they are done limiting you. It's time you stop giving excuses for them, and take God at His Word and become *"more than conquerors."* Are you willing to take the challenge? If you are, then there are great days ahead as you and God become *"more than conquerors"* together.

3

The Main Ingredient

My wife and daughter know that I love chocolate chip cookies. If either of them want to tug on my heart strings, they know that a batch of chocolate chip cookies will soften me up any time. The best type of chocolate chip cookies are the ones that you pull out of the oven before they are completely done. When you pull them out before they're done, they are still gooey on the inside, and it almost takes both hands to eat the cookie. There is nothing worse than looking forward to a chocolate chip cookie and finding out they are so hard that you can barely bite down on them.

In order to have a great chocolate chip cookie, there are some important ingredients that must be added. Inside of every chocolate chip cookie is flour, eggs, salt, baking soda, vanilla, milk, brown sugar, sugar and chocolate chips. Each of these ingredients are an important part of getting the taste that we desire. If I withhold one of these ingredients, it will change the taste of the chocolate chip cookie. It may still be a chocolate chip cookie, but it won't have the taste that I want it to have. Each ingredient plays an important part in creating the outcome I desire.

When we look at those who've overcome average, one may wonder what are the ingredients that helped them to overachieve? I can assure you every overachiever is different. Some are educated, and some have little to no education. You will find an overachiever in every race. Some overachievers have an outgoing personality while others are introverts. Some overachievers are good at public speaking, while others struggle to give a public address. Some overachievers grow up with both of their parents while others grow up in a single parent home. Some overachievers have a good background from whence they came while others grew up in broken homes. When it comes to the makeup of those who've overcome average, you will find that they come from all backgrounds, races and walks of life.

If I were to put my finger on the one ingredient that every overachiever has, that ingredient would be character. Where their weaknesses tried to hold them back, their character made up for their shortcomings and propelled them to overcome average. You will always find that every overachiever is a person of character. They may not have talent, but they have character. They may not have charisma, but they have character. They may not have the resources that others have, but they have character. Their character is what drives them from being average to overcoming average.

Psalm 15:4 rightly describes the character of those who overcome average when it says, *"In whose eyes a vile person is contemned; but he honoureth them that fear the LORD. He that sweareth to his own hurt, and changeth not."* Notice, character does right even though it may hurt them. Character doesn't hold its finger to the wind to find out what is popular at the moment; rather, character does right even when it hurts them or their prospects of success. Character helps a person overcome average because it becomes the moral fiber of who they are.

Character is who you are in private. This is where most who overcome average succeed, and where those who remain average fail. The average only wants to do things when they are noticed; whereas, the character of those who overcome average motivates them to do right simply because it is the right thing to do.

Three famous men who overcame average in the Scriptures are Shadrach, Meshach and Abednego. These three men exemplified character. They were hundreds of miles away from home. Their parents were not there to demand that they live right. Their priest was not there to correct them if they bowed to Nebuchadnezzar's golden image. These three young men were all alone and could get away with anything. Yet, when faced with the opportunity to do wrong, they did right even to their own detriment. When given another chance to bow to the image, they said, *"...O Nebuchadnezzar, we are not careful to answer thee in this matter. If it be so, our God whom we serve is able to deliver us from the burning fiery furnace, and he will deliver us out of thine hand, O king. But if not, be it known unto thee, O king, that we will not serve thy gods, nor worship the golden image which thou hast set up."* (Daniel 3:16-18) This is character on display. They didn't worry about the result; they were concerned with the action of doing right.

You will never overcome average without character. If there is any ingredient you need to develop in your life, it is the ingredient of character. You may rise for a short while without character, but your success will be short lived. Character may not bring immediate success, but it will develop the moral fiber of who you are so that when success is presented to you, you will already be doing what you are supposed to do. Character is the main ingredient you must have if you want to overcome average. Let me give you some thoughts about character that will be helpful to you.

1. Character is earned not inherited.

Just because a person's parents have character does not mean they will inherit it. Proverbs 20:21 says, *"An inheritance may be gotten hastily at the beginning; but the end thereof shall not be blessed."* Character is something that is earned. I like to put it this way, character is developed over time. Yes, you can learn from the character of your parents or leaders, but they cannot pass it down to you.

One of the reasons character helps a person overcome average is because it is something that is done day in and day out. It is not a one and done action. A person who overcomes average doesn't expect someone to hand them success; rather, their character tells them to do what they are supposed to do over time to earn success.

2. Character is doing the hard thing.

A person of character is never looking for the easy way; instead, they are looking to do right. Proverbs 22:13 says, *"The slothful man saith, There is a lion without, I shall be slain in the streets."* The slothful man is a classic underachiever. One of the reasons he underachieves is because he doesn't want to do what is hard. He wants everything in life to be easy.

The person who overcomes average is one who doesn't wait for everything to fall into place before they start doing what they are supposed to do. They do what they are supposed to do even when it is difficult. Part of the overachiever's character is finding a way to do something when difficulties come. It's not always going to be easy to tell the truth, but character tells the truth even when it hurts. It's not always easy to get up early in the morning, but character kicks you out of bed when you've only had two or three hours of sleep the night before because you have responsibilities that must be fulfilled. A person who overcomes average overachieves because they have the character to do what is hard while the average is at home waiting for everything to be easy. If you are waiting for everything to be easy in life, then you will never overcome average.

3. Character focuses on the action and not the result.

One of the most important qualities of an overachiever's character is that they are not result oriented; instead, they are action oriented. When Job faced the multiple calamities in his life, his wife came to him and said in Job 2:9, *"Then said his wife unto him, Dost thou still retain thine integrity? curse God, and die."* Job's wife was indicating that he would not change who he was though the results could be different if he did. In fact, Job backed this up when he said in Job 13:15, *"Though he slay me, yet will I trust in him: but I will maintain mine own ways before him."* Job was not focused on results. He was focused on doing right at all times, even when those times were not easy, and that was a direct result of his character.

If you are going to overcome average, then you must focus your character on doing right. Results don't make something right. What helps a person overcome average is that they do what is right when others won't do right. This is what separates those who overcome average from the average. The character of those who overcome average is more concerned with doing right than they are with the results. The character of those who overcome average does not determine what they will do based upon the result, instead they determine what they will do based upon what is right. Proverbs 11:3 makes this clear when it says, *"The integrity of the upright shall guide them: but the perverseness of transgressors shall destroy them."* Those who overcome average are guided by principles, and not by results and feelings.

4. Character always remembers there is a tomorrow.

One of the most important things about the character of those who overcome average is that they realize there are consequences to every action. Proverbs 22:1 says, *"A good name is rather to be chosen than great riches, and loving favour rather than silver and gold."* Character will be concerned with keeping a good name.

You will never overcome average by being an opportunist. Opportunists will do anything for the moment if it brings success, but they soon realize it could very likely soil their name. Friend, you have one name, and gaining success at the cost of losing that good name is not worth it. Having your character in tact at the end of life is more important than having temporary success.

When you look at those who overcome average, you will always find the main ingredient they all have is character. You may not be considered intelligent, but you can always have character. You may not have the background that others have, but you can still have character. You may not have the financial backing that others have, but you can still have character. If you don't become a person of character, then you will never find yourself overcoming average. Part of overcoming average is keeping your character while overcoming the obstacles of opportunity. I encourage you to work on your character. Be who you are supposed to be and stop worrying about success. You will find that character and overcoming average are married to each other. You won't have one without the other.

4

RUNNING ON 110 OR 220

In the early years of my ministry, my wife and I did not have a home. When I married her, I was already in evangelism, and the only thing we had was a Silverado pickup truck with a camper shell on the back. Literally, all of our possessions were in the back of a truck. God was very good to us and kept our possessions from being stolen.

One of our dreams in those early years was to have a fifth-wheel trailer that we could call home. We prayed for a trailer for about a year, and God graciously answered our prayers. God enabled us to get a 35' fifth wheel trailer with two slide-outs. One slide-out was in the bedroom area, and the other was in the living and dining room area. We thought we were in Heaven. To no longer have to sleep in the spare room of someone's house, or in a prophets chamber that was dirty and more of an afterthought was simply heaven. Not only did we not have to share a home, but we also were able to use our own washer and dryer because they fitted this trailer with a stackable washer and dryer.

Within the first week of owning the trailer, we encountered what we thought was a power problem.

When we purchased the trailer, they had an adaptor on the plug of the trailer that could plug into a 110 adaptor on the wall. Every time we tried to use more than one appliance at the same time, we kicked a breaker in the church. It became very unpleasant to have to run into the church to find the circuit breaker box and turn the breaker back on.

We quickly learned how to juggle our appliances so that we would not kick the breaker. If I was at the dining table and my wife wanted to use the washer, she asked me to turn off the air conditioner or not to use the microwave so that we could get our clothes washed. If I wanted to heat some water to make hot tea, I would ask her to turn off the washer until I was done heating the water. It really became a joke with us that the trailer couldn't do more than one thing at a time.

I was preaching in Arkansas, and there was an electrician in the church I was preaching at. I told the electrician our problem and asked him if he could help. He came to the trailer the next day to see if he could find out why we couldn't use more than one appliance at a time in this brand new trailer. He first checked my circuit breaker box in the trailer. Next, he looked at the plug that came out of the breaker box. He scratched his head a bit, and then rubbed his chin and finally he said to me, "Bro. Domelle, I believe I know why you can't use two appliances at the same time." He said, "You have been running this trailer on 110, when you should be using 220." We went down to the store and purchased some breakers and a large extension so that we could wire the trailer straight into the breaker box at the church. That first night my wife and I had a good time. We turned every appliance on and off multiple times because we were so excited about being able to use more than one appliance at a time.

Our problem was very simple, we were running the trailer on less than what it needed. The trailer couldn't perform to its fullest potential because we were only running it on half of the power that it could use. Once we plugged the trailer into 220, we were able to see how the trailer was intended to be used by the manufacturer.

This is the reason many Christians underachieve today. Many Christians are running on 110, when they could be running on 220. The only reason they don't overcome average is because they are missing the main ingredient to help them hit the potential God intends for them to reach. That ingredient that they are missing is the power of the Holy Spirit.

Many Christians are running on their own power, and that is why they are not able to do what God wants them to do. Many Christians settle for the average Sunday school class because they just think they can't do anymore. Many pastors settle for the average church because they have tried every method and system to no avail. Many bus workers are missing out on reaching a great amount of children because they have adapted to running on 110. Many soul winners accept coming back with nobody saved because they are trying to do God's work on 110. Many ministry workers are frustrated with their Christian life because all they seem to reap are average results. What is the problem? The problem is that they are running on 110 when they should be running on 220.

God says in John 14:12, *"Verily, verily, I say unto you, He that believeth on me, the works that I do shall he do also; and greater works than these shall he do; because I go unto my Father."* Notice, God says that we can do greater works that He did. In other words, we can see more people saved than Jesus did while He was on this Earth. We can help comfort more people than Jesus did. We can build greater works than Jesus. Wow, what a promise!

What is it that helps us to do these greater works? God tells us in John 14:16 when He says, *"And I will pray the Father, and he shall give you another Comforter, that he may abide with you for ever;"* When Jesus went to Heaven, that allowed the Holy Spirit of God to indwell the believer. We now have another power inside of us that we can access so that we can do all that God intends for us to do. Instead of running on 110, we can run on 220 by having the Holy Spirit empower us.

Friend, you don't have to be average or below average. You have inside of you the power that will help you to overcome average. That power is the power of the Holy Spirit of God. There is only one reason you are not on your way to overcoming average, and that is because you are not accessing the power to help you become an overachiever. You can try to do the works of God on your own and fail, or with the power of God you can do more than you ever imagined.

When you consider who God used in the Scriptures, you must admit that many of them overcame average. They said about Peter in Acts 4:13, *"Now when they saw the boldness of Peter and John, and perceived that they were unlearned and ignorant men, they marvelled; and they took knowledge of them, that they had been with Jesus."* He had no knowledge of his own that caused him to overcome average, but he spent time with Jesus and had God's power on his life, and that is what allowed him to overcome average.

The Apostle Paul no doubt overcame average. When Paul described his talents he said in 1 Corinthians 15:9, *"For I am the least of the apostles, that am not meet to be called an apostle, because I persecuted the church of God."* When he described his personality he said in 2 Corinthians 11:6, *"But though I be rude in speech, yet not in knowledge; but we have been throughly made manifest among you in all things."* It was only the power of God's Holy Spirit that helped him to overcome average.

Paul tells us expressly where he received power to overcome average in Romans 15:18-19 when he says, *"For I will not dare to speak of any of those things which Christ hath not wrought by me, to make the Gentiles obedient, by word and deed, Through mighty signs and wonders, by the power of the Spirit of God; so that from Jerusalem, and round about unto Illyricum, I have fully preached the gospel of Christ."* Paul acknowledged that he could not have done the works he did by himself, but he said that every mighty sign and wonder that was done through him was done because of the power of the Holy Spirit.

When you look at the church in the Book of Acts, there is no question how this group of one hundred and twenty people turned the world upside down for Christ. It all started in an upper room. They were in that room praying, and in Acts 2:4 God said something happened to them, *"And they were all filled with the Holy Ghost, and began to speak with other tongues, as the Spirit gave them utterance."* That filling of the Holy Ghost is what took a bunch of average people and turned them into overachievers so that they could turn a world upside down for Christ.

You will never overcome average without the main ingredient of God's power on your life. God promised to give you His power in Acts 1:8 when He says, *"But ye shall receive power, after that the Holy Ghost is come upon you..."* Friend, you can try to run your life, marriage, home, ministry and business on 110 and fail because you don't have the amount of power needed. The only way you will ever overcome average in any of these areas is to be sure to get the main ingredient in your life, and that ingredient is God's power. You can settle for less and be average, or you can yield to the Holy Spirit of God every day of your life and ask Him for His power to help you to do what others thought you could not do.

So, what are you going to do? Are you going to continue juggling the average by running on 110, or are you going to get the 220 power of the Holy Spirit and overcome average? It is up to you. If you choose 110 and run everything in your power, then you will quickly become frustrated; however, if you get God's power on your life, you will quickly find that His power will lift you to overcome average. I challenge you today to daily take time to ask God to empower you in every task you do. Yield yourself to Him and allow Him to lead you through His power.

5

GET UP

It is 6 AM, and the alarm goes off. You know you need to get up, but you are just too tired to pull yourself out of bed. Out of habit, you reach over to the alarm clock and hit the snooze button so you can sleep just a bit longer. Five minutes later, it goes off again. Again, you have the same reaction and hit the snooze button. Finally, it hits you, you're running late. You jump out of bed and quickly get ready for the day, but now you don't have time to read the Scriptures or pray. This is the normal morning routine of many average people.

Those who overcome average overachieve because they get up when others won't. There will be mornings when the overachiever is tired and worn out, but they get up because they have work that needs to be done. There are mornings when the overachiever doesn't feel good, but they get up because they have responsibilities that must get done. It is no secret why those who overcome average achieve when you consider that day in and day out they get up in spite of how tired they are or how they feel.

For instance, let's say there are two people who desire to go into business. They both have everything in common. Their location is exactly the same. Their personalities are exactly alike. Their financial backing is completely the same. If you were to look at them, there would be no difference. Yet, one succeeds and the other fails. The one who fails realizes they are their own boss, and they know that they can open their business at any time they desire. One morning they are especially tired, so they decide to sleep in and open later. Another day they are not feeling well, so they don't open their business that day. The one who succeeds gets up every morning at the same time and goes to work no matter how they feel or how tired they are. The one who gets up in spite of feelings succeeds while the other does not. The one is considered a person who overcame average, while the other is considered an underachiever. The only difference is one gets up every morning no matter how they feel.

Those who overcome average exceed expectations because they get up every morning. Proverbs 6:10-11 says, *"Yet a little sleep, a little slumber, a little folding of the hands to sleep: So shall thy poverty come as one that travelleth, and thy want as an armed man."* The sluggard is an underachiever, and God shows us that one of the reasons they underachieve is because they sleep too much. They want to sleep a little more. They want to rest just a bit longer. They allow their body to tell them what to do and not their responsibilities. Those who overcome average always do what they are supposed to do in spite of how much sleep they've had.

One of the keys to overcoming average is determined by your morning habits. You show me what your morning habits are, and I will show you the degree of your achievement. It doesn't matter what your excuse may be, your morning habits will dictate how much you achieve in life. Let me give you several thoughts about getting up early every morning.

1. You're always going to be tired.

One of the reasons people have a hard time getting up is because they feel tired. Let's be honest with ourselves. It really doesn't matter how much sleep you get, you are always going to be tired. This is why you need to get up every morning in spite of how you feel.

Proverbs 6:6 says, *"Go to the ant, thou sluggard; consider her ways, and be wise:"* When you study the ant, you will see the ant is up and going at the break of day. That is why they make it through the winter time. Imagine if the ant was tired one morning and slept in, or the next morning didn't feel well, so both mornings it slept in. If the ant did that, it would not have enough food in the cold of winter.

Being tired is a part of life. Those who are the greatest achievers are those who get up when they don't feel like it. Get the sleep you need, and then get up. Accept the fact that you are always going to be tired, so get up even when you are tired.

2. Ask God to help you get up.

Matthew 7:7-8 says, *"Ask, and it shall be given you; seek, and ye shall find; knock, and it shall be opened unto you: For every one that asketh receiveth; and he that seeketh findeth; and to him that knocketh it shall be opened."* If you are having a problem getting up every morning, then you ought to ask God the night before to help you to get up in the morning. Now, let me be blunt with you. God will wake you up, but He won't pull you out of bed. When God wakes you up, you have to have the character to get yourself out of bed.

3. Don't make provision to sleep in.

One of the greatest reasons we fail to get up is because we set ourselves up for failure. Romans 13:14 says, *"But put ye on the Lord Jesus Christ, and make not provision for the flesh, to fulfil the lusts thereof."* You will never succeed in getting up when you make provision to sleep in. When the alarm clock is next to your bed and you have the snooze button set to go off, you are making provision for the flesh.

Years ago I had a problem with sleeping in. I didn't sleep in till late morning, but I would get up around 8 every morning. I wanted to get up earlier, but I'd hit the snooze button about five or six times before finally realizing I was late for the day. I'd jump out of bed, and quickly get ready for the day, but I felt disgusted with myself because I didn't get out of bed when I should have. My way of overcoming this was to move my alarm clock under the desk in my room and turn off the snooze button. After a few mornings of knocking my head on the desk trying to turn the alarm clock off, I learned to get up in the morning. Now, I have no problem getting up early because I don't make provision for the flesh.

You must completely remove anything that gives you the opportunity to sleep in each morning. Get rid of the snooze button. Have an alarm clock that doesn't have a snooze button, or turn the one you have off. Also, don't set the alarm so close to bed. You fail to get up because it's too easy to turn off the alarm and roll over and go back to sleep. Furthermore, get up as soon as the alarm goes off. Don't fall for the trap that you'll sleep five more minutes and then get up. Train yourself to get up the first time the alarm clock sounds.

4. Go to bed earlier at night.

One of the secrets to getting up early is simply going to sleep earlier. If we're honest with ourselves, one of the main reasons we can't get up in the morning is because we go to bed too late. Go to bed earlier and you will find that it is much easier to get up early in the morning.

5. Plan important tasks early in the morning.

One of the things that helps me get up in the mornings is that I plan many tasks earlier in the morning. When you have to do something first thing in the morning, you will find that it is much easier to get up. Eighty-six times the word *"early"* is used in the Scriptures. God is teaching you to start doing things early in the morning. If you do so, you'll find the battle to get up is much easier. If you plan everything late in the day, then there is no purpose in getting up early. Plan the most important tasks earlier in the morning, and you'll find that your mind will wake you up.

6. Make getting up early a habit.

One of the mistakes people make is they only get up on the days they "have to" get up. This is a mistake because you need to make getting up a habit. When it becomes a habit, you won't even have to think about it.

Romans 12:2 says, *"And be not conformed to this world: but be ye transformed by the renewing of your mind, that ye may prove what is that good, and acceptable, and perfect, will of God."* This verse is teaching that the way to get rid of bad habits is *"by the renewing of your mind."* In other words, you will only overcome bad habits by establishing good ones.

They say it takes twenty-one days to form a habit. That means for twenty-one days it is going to be difficult to establish the habit of getting up. During this time, determination is really going to have to become a part of your life. You must be determined to get up in the morning. One of the benefits of making this a habit is that it adds to your character. It will make you a better person, and your character will benefit from it.

7. Don't use the crutch, "I'm just not a morning person."

This is one of the most common excuses for not getting up in the morning. I've learned that it has nothing to do with being a morning person; it has everything to do with being lazy. If getting up is going to become a habit, then you must throw out any excuse and especially the excuse that you're not a morning person. Accept that you are trying to overcome laziness. If you throw this excuse out, then you are well on your way to getting up early every morning.

8. Don't let holidays and vacations break the habit.

I have personally made it a habit to get up the same time everyday no matter what day it is. If I'm on vacation, I get up the same time I always get up. When it is a holiday, I get up at the same time. Don't allow holidays and vacations get you out of the routine of getting up. All it takes is one day of getting out of your routine of getting up, and you could easily slip back into the bad habit of sleeping in.

9. Take a nap if you must.

Okay, so you're tired, then take a nap. Many great overachievers in the past took a nap everyday. Dr. John R. Rice and Dr. Lee Roberson took a nap everyday. These men were great men, but instead of sleeping in when they were tired, they got up and worked until early afternoon, and at that time they took a short nap. You are not lazy or unspiritual by taking a nap. Jesus took a nap in Mark 4:38. It doesn't have to be long, but a short nap can add energy to your day. I get up early every morning, but nearly every afternoon I stop for about fifteen minutes for a nap. That nap gives me the energy I need for the remainder of the day.

10. Keep records of your progress to determine if change is needed.

Don't let your failure of sleeping in defeat you. When I was trying to overcome the habit of sleeping in, I kept daily records of my progress. I found that the records either encouraged or convicted me, depending upon how I did. You won't conquer this overnight, but by keeping records of how you're doing you will find it will help you to overcome the bad habit of sleeping in.

11. Don't do it all at once.

Another tip for helping you to get up earlier in the morning is to take little steps towards your ultimate goal. One of the principles you'll find in the Scriptures is that God allows us to grow little by little. Deuteronomy 7:22 says, *"And the LORD thy God will put out those nations before thee by little and little: thou mayest not consume them at once, lest the beasts of the field increase upon thee."* Notice, God allowed them to have small victories as they conquered Canaan.

Many people discourage themselves by trying to take the big step of getting up an hour to two hours earlier all at one time. Instead of trying to get up at your ultimate goal, why not work yourself there? Get up ten minutes earlier than what you usually do for a couple of days, and then move it another ten minutes and so on until you get to your desired time. By moving ten minutes at a time, you are allowing your body to adjust, and you are conquering small attainable goals on your way to the ultimate goal of getting up earlier every day.

Getting up early every morning is an important part of overcoming average. Anybody can get up earlier. It is a choice. Choose right now that you are going to take a step towards overcoming average by getting up earlier everyday.

For relevant articles that meet the daily Christian needs visit Oldpathsjournal.com.

6

FINISH WHAT YOU START

One thing that makes a person an overachiever is that they finish what they start. Many underachievers simply don't finish what they start. They may start many projects, but they never finish. You will never be an overachiever unless you learn to finish what you start.

When I was in high school, I was on the track team. My dad was our coach, and there were several rules he had for the team. One of the most important things he drilled into us was to finish the race at all costs. He used to tell us that if we don't finish the race, then they had better be carrying us off on a stretcher. I know that today that type of coaching seems to be a thing of the past, but that type of coaching is what taught us to finish what we started.

One of the events I ran was the 200 meter dash. This was just about the farthest distance that I was good at because of my height. The events that were longer than that normally were ran better by those whose legs were longer. One day while I was getting ready for my event, they announced the event was coming up. I went through my stretches, and practiced my start. Finally, it was time for the race. I put my starting blocks down in my lane, and got into my starting position. It wasn't long before the starting gun went off and we were literally off to the races. In the 200 meter dash, you go through one turn before you are on the final straightway toward the finish line. As I was went through the turn, I felt a sharp pain on the ball of my right foot. Every time I put my foot down, the pain seemed to get worse. I kept on running because I remembered my dad's words, "The only reason you don't finish a race is because they are carrying you off on a stretcher." I finished the race and fell down on the track. I pulled my shoe off and I saw that my sock was covered in blood. When I pulled my sock off, I noticed some skin that had pulled off the ball of my foot from a blister, and it left my foot bleeding.

My dad saw me sitting on the track at the finish line, and he ran over and asked me if I was okay. I showed him my foot, and he immediately got the first aid kit and had someone clean my foot and wrap it so it wouldn't get worse. After they were done, my father asked me why I kept running. I told him that he always taught us to finish the race, and that I didn't need to be carried off on a stretcher, so I finished. He commended me for not allowing a small injury to keep me from finishing. I learned a very valuable lesson from track that I have carried with me my entire life, and that lesson is to finish what you start.

Many of the characters in the Scriptures finished what they started. The Apostle Paul said in 2 Timothy 4:7, *"I have fought a good fight, I have finished my course, I have kept the faith:"* Though he faced several obstacles that tried to keep him from finishing, he still finished what he started. Many would consider him an overachiever, and I believe one of the reasons is because he finished what he started. Jesus said in John 19:30, *"...It is finished: and he bowed his head, and gave up the ghost."* If our Saviour saw the importance of finishing, then you should see the importance of it. Finishing what you start is an important key to overcoming average.

Proverbs 10:26 says, *"As vinegar to the teeth, and as smoke to the eyes, so is the sluggard to them that send him."* The sluggard is a classic underachiever. You will notice that the sluggard is not dependable when given an errand because they don't finish what they start. They may start the project, but you can be sure that they won't finish it.

We live in times when we excuse people for not finishing. If they give a good excuse, then we pass it off and excuse them. Parents today are often guilty of letting their children not finish what they start. They then wonder why their children don't achieve much in life. A key to overcoming average is being a finisher. If you start something, then you need to be sure to finish it. Let me give you several thoughts on how to finish what you start.

1. Don't let your eyes get bigger than your stomach.

One of the reasons we struggle in finishing what we start is because we start too many things. One of the rules we had at my home growing up was that we had to eat whatever was put on our plate. We would often see something we liked, and it was common that we started putting more on the plate than what my mom knew we could finish. She would say, "Son, don't let your eyes get bigger than your stomach." In other words, she was telling me not to put more on my plate than I could handle. Only take the portion that I knew I could eat, and if I wanted more, then I could add more later.

When it comes to taking on projects, it can be easy to let our eyes get bigger than our stomach. We keep on taking projects, and before long we have so many projects that we are not finishing any of them. Many times a project will pull on our heart strings, and we take it on only to find ourselves overloaded and not able to finish.

Philippians 3:13-14 says, *"Brethren, I count not myself to have apprehended: but this one thing I do, forgetting those things which are behind, and reaching forth unto those things which are before, I press toward the mark for the prize of the high calling of God in Christ Jesus."* God is teaching that one of the best ways to finish what we start is to do one thing at a time. Paul pressed forward by doing one thing. You will have an easier time finishing what you start if you will learn to narrow down the projects you start, and only working on them one at a time. Let me assure you that there is nothing wrong with telling someone you are not capable of taking on a project. If you are already overloaded, then politely refuse a project so that you can finish what you have already started.

2. Don't let obstacles stop your progress.

Anytime you start a project, you can expect obstacles to come and try to keep you from finishing. When obstacles come, you must not let them keep you from progress. Progress is the key to finishing. Those who overcome average don't look at obstacles; instead, they look at opportunities to help them be a better finisher.

Romans 12:21 says, *"Be not overcome of evil, but overcome evil with good."* Those who overcome average will not let the obstacles overcome them, rather they will overcome the obstacles. Those who overcome average understand that they must not let their progress stop. They understand that they must keep on going when they face great obstacles. Those who overcome average understand that they must keep progress moving if they are going to finish what they start.

3. Don't let failure dictate the finishing point.

Failure is a part of life, but failure must not be the dictator of the finish line. Just because you have failed does not mean you are finished. Those who overcome average never allow failure to define the finish. They get back up after failure.

Proverbs 24:16 says, *"For a just man falleth seven times, and riseth up again: but the wicked shall fall into mischief."* What I love about this verse is that the words *"seven times"* is referring to the seven days of the week. In other words the just man, or the one who overcomes average, failed seven straight days, but he got up the next week and kept going towards his goal. He did not allow his failure to dictate the finishing point. The difference between those who overcome average and the underachiever is that the overcomer gets up after a failure while the underachiever allows failure to keep him down.

4. Don't let weariness keep you from finishing.

One of the hardest things you will accomplish is to keep on going when you are tired. I often tell people the you have to keep putting one foot in front of the other when you are tired.

Galatians 6:9 says, *"And let us not be weary in well doing: for in due season we shall reap, if we faint not."* There is no doubt that those who overcome average get weary with doing right, but they keep on going until they finish. You may be weary of doing the right thing, but if you are going to overcome average, then you must keep going even when you don't feel like taking another step.

When you want to quit, just take another step. When you want to resign your church, keep on pastoring. When you want to quit your marriage, stay married. When you want to close your business, find a way to keep it open. When you are tired of being turned down, keep on inviting people and witnessing to people about Christ. Whatever your degree of weariness, you must keep going and don't let weariness keep you from finishing. The chance to overcome average is often one step past the quitting point.

5. Don't get sidetracked from what you started.

If you are going to finish what you start, then you must be careful about letting things sidetrack you from what you are supposed to be doing. Philippians 3:14 says, *"I press toward the mark for the prize of the high calling of God in Christ Jesus."* Pressing for the mark means that you keep your eyes focused on the finish line.

You will find there will be many good things with which you can be involved, but if it is not what God wants you to do, then don't let it sidetrack you. Throughout my ministry I have been offered many opportunities, but most of them had nothing to do with my calling. Though they were not bad things to do, I had to stay focused on what I was supposed to do. If you're not careful, you will get involved in so many things that you can't do any of them well. Don't let things of no consequence sidetrack you from what you're supposed to be doing.

6. Don't let casualties scare you from finishing.

2 Samuel 2:23 says, *"Howbeit he refused to turn aside: wherefore Abner with the hinder end of the spear smote him under the fifth rib, that the spear came out behind him; and he fell down there, and died in the same place: and it came to pass, that as many as came to the place where Asahel fell down and died stood still."* The people in this verse were fighting a battle, yet, every time someone came to where Asahel's body laid they stopped and looked which kept them from fighting the battle. Finally, someone removed the body so others would not stop as they fought.

You are going to find there are going to be casualties of war in every line of work. What you cannot do is allow the casualties to scare you away from finishing. You don't have to be a casualty, and if you are one, at least you went down fighting. I would rather be a casualty than a spectator. Don't let the failures of others scare you away from finishing.

7. Know the ins and outs of your project before starting.

Here is one of the most important keys to finishing. Knowing what you are getting yourself into is a key to finishing. Luke 14:28 says, *"For which of you, intending to build a tower, sitteth not down first, and counteth the cost, whether he have sufficient to finish it?"* God is teaching us to count the cost of anything before starting.

Before you start anything, take some time to study everything about your task so you will know what to expect. It is like having a game plan for a team. If you go into a game without a game plan, you are sure to lose. If you go into a project without a plan, you are sure to be unsuccessful. Those who overcome average succeed because they counted the cost of a project before they started.

8. Don't be afraid to make adjustments.

One thing about those who overcome average is they are not afraid to make adjustments when they see that something is not working right. A losing coach will go in at halftime and make adjustments to their game plan, but they rarely forsake the initial game plan. You must not be afraid to make adjustments to what you are doing. Don't be so stubborn that you keep doing something that is not working just because you have always done it. Those who overcome average will swallow their pride and acknowledge they need to make adjustments, but their adjustments don't mean they have forsaken their game plan.

9. Don't let time keep you from finishing.

I read a story about a lady who for thirty years pursued a college degree in history. The story went on to say that this lady, at age 95, walked across the platform and received her college degree at the same time her granddaughter received her college degree. What I love about this story is that this lady did not let time squelch her dream of a degree, instead she kept on studying until she finished her degree even though she was 95 years of age.

Don't ever allow time to keep you from finishing. If you have been doing something for a long period of time, then keep doing it until you finish. Those who overcome average don't quit until they are finished. It may take them thirty years like this lady, but they will finish.

10. Finishing is the only option.

Jesus said in John 19:30, *"...It is finished: and he bowed his head, and gave up the ghost."* Jesus kept going until He finished. Finishing was the only option He had, and that is why many considered Him an overachiever in His day.

Those who overcome average never start something they don't finish. Finishing is the key to overcoming average, because finishing will put you ahead of most people. If you are going to overcome average, then you must decide that you will finish everything that you start. There is no other option but to finish. Make it a part of your character to finish what you start, and you will be one step closer to overcoming average.

Sign up for
Daily Devotionals
at Oldpathsjournal.com

7

CLAIMING YOUR STAKE

Growing up in a home that did not have much money allowed me to learn a very valuable lesson as a young man. I was taught from an early age that if I wanted something then I needed to work to get it. My parents didn't give me an allowance for doing my chores around the house, for they felt an allowance was simply teaching me to always expect handouts.

When I hit the magical 15 years of age, my parents allowed me to get my drivers permit, and I was later able to get my drivers license. My father told me early on that he was not going to purchase a car for me. He told me that if I wanted a car, then I would have to purchase one for myself. This motivated me to not only work hard to earn the money to purchase a car, but it also motivated me to save money so I could purchase a car. It also taught me to appreciate what I had once I purchased it.

Everything I own today I have purchased with my own money that I earned through working and saving. My parents didn't give me one penny to purchase a car. They didn't help me in the purchase of my home. It wasn't that they didn't love me, it was all about teaching me the principle of working for what I get instead of having my hand out expecting everyone else to pay my way.

Nobody will overcome average with their hand out waiting for someone else to pay their way. We live in days where people have become entitlement happy. Sadly, many Christians have learned to be beggars with their hands out waiting for someone to pay their way instead of figuring out a way to pray down what they need or work for it and save money. Christians have learned how to whine about their needs instead of going to God to ask Him to supply their needs. Instead of claiming their stake and deciding to work for what they get, many have depended upon the government and others to provide for them.

If you are going to overcome average, then you are going to have to claim your stake and work for what you get. You will find that those who are above average learned the value of hard work. They didn't stand on the side of the street begging for money. They worked long hours and saved their money to get what they have. They didn't look to the government to give them what they have; rather, they worked for it. Because they claimed their stake and worked for what they have, they appreciate what they have and take better care of it.

God says in Proverbs 13:4, *"The soul of the sluggard desireth, and hath nothing: but the soul of the diligent shall be made fat."* The sluggard is too lazy to go out and work for what they want. The sluggard sits and desires waiting for someone to give to them, but they never obtain. On the other hand, the diligent also desires, but he goes and works for his desire and obtains it. The diligent claims his stake and finds a way to get it. It all comes down to one having their hand out waiting for someone else to give it to them, while the other works hard, saves and finds a way to get what they desire. Once the diligent have what they desire, they keep on doing what they did to get it and add to their supply over and over again. Thus, they are made *"fat."*

You have a choice in life to either feel you are entitled to certain things and believe it should be given to you, or you can claim your stake and rise above the average and get what you go after. As long as you have your hand out, you will continue to underachieve. Those who overcome average are those who learn to work for what they get. Let me give you some thoughts on how to claim your stake.

1. Take smaller portions and save the rest for later.

When I was a boy, my mother taught me the importance taking smaller portions. She used to tell me that I could always get seconds if I wanted more. Instead of taking more than I needed, the smaller portion rule saved me from taking too much.

This is a good principle by which to live if you are going to claim your stake. The problem with the sluggard in Proverbs 13:4 is that he wanted more than he could truly handle. He simply didn't need everything he desired. If the sluggard had kept his desires in proportion, then he may have had the initiative to work for it.

I'm afraid that we have become so wrapped up in things in life that our appetite for material things is too big. The average politician knows that they can be elected if they promise to give more entitlements than their opponent. It is sad, but this has created an entitlement mentality.

You need to become content with what you have. God commands, *"Let your conversation be without covetousness; and be content with such things as ye have..."* (Hebrews 13:5) If you don't fall in love with things, you will find it will be easier to work for what you want and have.

2. Don't expect anything from anyone, and everything you do get will be a bonus.

Let me make this clear to you, nobody owes you anything! We get the mentality that everyone owes us something; therefore, we have our hand out waiting for them to give it to us. God says in 2 Thessalonians 3:12, *"Now them that are such we command and exhort by our Lord Jesus Christ, that with quietness they work, and eat their own bread."* Notice that God says, *"...eat their own bread."* Stop looking to eat of something for which someone else worked. Look at your own plate and eat off it. Just because someone has more than you does not mean they owe you a bite. If you don't expect anyone to give you a bite of what they have, then when they do give you a bite it will become a bonus. However, once they give you a bite, don't believe they owe you another bite of what they have the next time. If you want something then work to put it on your own plate.

3. You are responsible for yourself.

God says, *"So then every one of us shall give account of himself to God."* (Romans 14:12) Nobody is responsible to give to you. You give account of yourself. You are to work for your own bread. Your parents don't owe you a college education. Your parents don't owe you a car or a house. The wealthy are not responsible to provide for you. You are responsible to yourself and God. When you realize you are responsible for yourself, then you will start working for what you have.

4. Save for later.

One of the problems of entitlement happy people is that they want everything now and won't save something for later in life. One of the invaluable principles I learned many years ago is that I need to learn to save some things for later in life. If I enjoy everything now, then I won't have anything to enjoy later in life. This kept me from wanting everyone to give me something.

You are going to get older in life. If everyone does everything for you now, then what will you have to work for or to look forward to later? Part of claiming your stake is realizing that if you can't afford it now, then you will save that for later when you can afford it. Develop the principle in your life that if you can't afford it then you will not look to others to give it to you, but you will wait until you have found a way to work and obtain it.

5. Ask God if you need it.

God promised in Philippians 4:19, *"But my God shall supply all your need according to his riches in glory by Christ Jesus."* Part of our problem in claiming our stake is that we run to people with our hand out instead of running to God Who can truly help us. God promised to supply our need, so if we truly need something, He will supply it.

I have found that most of the time God supplies our need through hard work. God supplied the Promised Land to Israel, but they had to work to get it. God supplied everything for Adam and Eve, but they had to work to get it. God told them in Genesis 1:28, *"And God blessed them, and God said unto them, Be fruitful, and multiply, and replenish the earth, and subdue it: and have dominion over the fish of the sea, and over the fowl of the air, and over*

every living thing that moveth upon the earth."
Notice, God gave them the Earth, but they had to
subdue it. Subduing the Earth took work.

You should never run to people; you should run to
God. When you run to God, you will often find out
that when He supplies your need He will still require
you to work to get it. Those who overcome average
are not afraid to ask God to supply their need
because they are not afraid to work.

6. Work harder.

If you are going to overcome average, then you
are going to have to work harder than the average.
What separates the average from those who
overcome average is their work ethic. Most of the
time those who are above average are simply those
who worked harder than the average.

David was one of many brethren, but the reason
he rose above his brethren was because he was
working while they were at home. Elisha wasn't the
only young man whom God could have used to
succeed Elijah, but what separated him from the rest
was that he worked. Elijah found Elisha in the field
working. It was probably his work ethic that qualified
him to succeed.

You will never overcome average if you work with
the same intensity as the average. The average work
forty hours a week, while those who overcome average

work sixty or more hours a week. The average have an average work ethic while those who overcome average work harder and longer than anyone else. Those who overcome average arrive before the average show up and they stay after the average go home. It truly has nothing to do with talent, but it has much to do with who works the hardest.

7. Learn the value of saving.

If you are going to claim your stake, then you must learn the value of saving. Look again at Proverbs 13:4, *"The soul of the sluggard desireth, and hath nothing: but the soul of the diligent shall be made fat."* Notice that the diligent *"shall be made fat."* In other words, they worked and saved, which eventually allowed them to have more than the rest. If they spent everything they earned, then they would have never had the excess.

Part of overcoming average is learning the value of saving. Don't use something just because you have it. You might want to save it for the day you need it. Those who overcome average are not always people who get everything at one time, but they are patient enough to work and save a little at a time. Then one day they end up having more than the average. You will never have excess in life if you use something up as soon as you get it.

Those who overcome average are those who gain wisdom and knowledge a little at a time and save it up until they have more wisdom and knowledge than others. The person who is financially above average oftentimes is not one who makes more money, they just learned the value of saving. While others spent, they put money into the bank and investments. They didn't wait for someone to give them a windfall of money, they just saved a little bit every time they got money, and eventually they had more than the average.

Friend, overcoming average will not happen if you wait for people to give to you. You will overcome average when you make a decision to take personal responsibility by working for everything you get. The benefit of working for what you get is that it brings true satisfaction because you acquired what you have. Don't be one who waits with their hand out. Be the one who works harder than anyone else, and you will find yourself overcoming average.

8

FIND A WAY

We live in a generation that seems to have lost its determination and creativity when it comes to finding a way to do what needs to get done. The generation in which we live is filled with excuses as to why things can't be done. There used to be a time when people would step up to the plate and take personal responsibility instead of making excuses. Instead, today we have become an excuse driven society that always finds a reason as to why something can't be done instead of finding a way to get it done.

One of the things my parents drilled inside of me was the determination to find a way to get something done. I remember watching my father work on cars and getting to a point where he was stuck and not sure how to move forward. I watched him as he analyzed the problem, and then came up with a solution to fix the situation. That creativity in my father caused me to be a solutions oriented person. Instead of looking at a problem and saying it can't be done, I've determined to find a solution to the situation and fix it. I refuse to let a difficult situation keep me from accomplishing something.

One of the chores I had as a teenage boy was pulling weeds in the flower bed. I hated this chore with a passion. About once a month my mother would tell me that she wanted me to go pull the weeds out of the flower bed. It never failed that I would come across one weed that seemed to have a root that grew all the way to China. It didn't matter how hard I pulled, that root wouldn't come out. Instead of figuring out a way to pull the root up, I would simply pull the leaves off the root and cover the root with dirt.

When I went into the house and informed my mother that I was done, she would proceed to go outside to see how good of a job I did. It seemed to never fail, and to this day I don't know how she did it, but she would find that one root that I couldn't pull out. She would say to me, "Son, I thought you said you pulled the weeds." I always responded, "I did." She then pointed out the root that I covered and told me that the job was not done until the root was pulled. I would tell her that the root wouldn't come out no matter what I did. She then would say, "Son, figure out a way. Don't let the root win." My mother was teaching me not to give an excuse; instead, I needed to find a way to get the job done.

Those who overcome average are those who don't give excuses. Those who overcome average have a deep determination that one way or another they will find a way to make it happen. It doesn't matter how hard it may be, how long it will take or how many resources they need, they simply find a way to get the job done without excuses.

Proverbs 20:4 says, *"The sluggard will not plow by reason of the cold; therefore shall he beg in harvest, and have nothing."* The sluggard always has an excuse as to why they can't do something. It's either too cold to reap the harvest or it's too hot. Instead of figuring out a way to endure the cold, the sluggard simply sits in the comforts of his house not realizing that leads to poverty.

On the other hand, the diligent find a way to make things happen. Proverbs 10:4 says, *"He becometh poor that dealeth with a slack hand: but the hand of the diligent maketh rich."* You will notice that while the one gives excuses, the diligent finds a way to make riches. Excuse making leads to poverty while finding a way leads to profit and success. Both are faced with obstacles, but the diligent are those who overcome average by finding a way to overcome their obstacles.

There are several excuses people give in life. Excuses truly are all the same. They are just clothed differently. Let me show you how you should respond to each excuse that you may want to give.

1. Accept responsibility and move on.

One of the biggest problems we face today is people blame someone else or something else for why they have done. Those who overcome average accept personal responsibility for what they have done, and then they move on. You can blame someone for your mistakes or you can accept the blame and move on.

In the Garden of Eden, Adam and Eve used this excuse. Notice what they said, *"And the man said, The woman whom thou gavest to be with me, she gave me of the tree, and I did eat. And the Lord God said unto the woman, What is this that thou hast done? And the woman said, The serpent beguiled me, and I did eat."* (Genesis 3:12-13) Instead of accepting responsibility for what they did, they played the blame game.

You can blame other people for your failures, or you can accept responsibility and move on to overcome average. You can blame circumstances and surroundings for your failures, or you can find a way to overcome them and become victorious. You will only overcome average when you decide to take personal responsibility for your failures and move on.

2. Stop putting things off! Now is the best time.

Another excuse we like to use is that the timing isn't right. You find this excuse used in the parable of the Great Supper. All three people who were invited to the Great Supper gave the excuse that the timing was not right.

66

Those who overcome average will stop waiting for the perfect time and just start doing what they are supposed to do. There are many people waiting for the perfect time to go into the ministry, while others went into the ministry and found a way to work out the timing. Timing is a poor excuse that will always be accessible. My question to you is this, when is the right time? You have used this excuse long enough. If you are going to overcome average, you need to find a way to make this the right time to make things happen.

3. I might fail!

One of the greatest excuses people use is that they don't want to fail. I have news for you, nobody wants to fail. I'm reminded of the disciples in the boat when Jesus said, *"Come."* All the disciples heard Jesus give the command, but only one stepped out in spite of the fear of failure. By the way, he did fail, but he overcame his failure.

Let me just say that you are going to fail. Get over it! Those who have overcome average didn't overcome average by never failing. No, they overcame average by getting up after they failed. They failed time and time again, but they kept going. They knew when they stepped out that they would fail, but that didn't stop them. You will never overcome average if you let fear stop you from stepping out. Stop worrying about failure. Deal with failure when it comes, but step out.

4. I'm not smart enough!

Another excuse people use is that they are not smart enough to do something. You must realize that you will never be smart enough to do something until you are done. Those who think they know everything before they start are usually those who become the greatest flops. It is those who took what knowledge they had and stepped out who've overcome average.

In the Book of Proverbs, God talks about understanding many times. You will always find that understanding comes after having the wisdom to step out and trust God. Wisdom is doing what you know you are supposed to do, but understanding is having the wherewithal to explain how it's done. That is only accomplished by finding a way.

Instead of waiting until you have the "know how" to do everything, step out and use what you do know, and God will give you the understanding and the knowledge for the rest as you need it. God promises, *"But my God shall supply all your need according to his riches in glory by Christ Jesus."* (Philippians 4:19) God's promise to supply your need also applies to knowledge, so step out and find a way by trusting God to give you the knowledge when you need it. Those who overcome average do not wait until they are smart enough. They trust God by faith that He will give them the wisdom they need when it is needed.

5. I'm just not the right age.

Age has always been a great excuse as to why a person can't do something. They are either too old or too young. Using age as an excuse is simply telling God that He is not strong enough to help you overcome the age barrier.

When Sarah thought that she was too old to have a child, God asked her, *"Is any thing too hard for the Lord?"* (Genesis 18:14) Saul said to David when he was about to face Goliath, *"Thou art not able to go against this Philistine to fight with him: for thou art but a youth..."* (1 Samuel 17:33) In both cases age was a poor excuse, for God came through on both.

Your age is not an obstacle with God. The only one who is making an obstacle out of your age is you. You can let your age be the excuse to be average, or you can overcome your age and do something great for God. Don't let age be your excuse. Realize God is very capable of using you no matter your age.

6. The glass is half empty.

The average will always have a pessimistic attitude. You will find that the average always says it can't be done. That is what makes them average. Average always looks at the difficulty instead of looking for creative ways to make it work.

The one who overcomes average is simply more creative than the average. When Moses and the

Children of Israel faced the Red Sea, they had a God Who was creative. Instead of saying they couldn't do it, God parted the Red Sea and made a way. When they came to the Jordan River and couldn't find a way to get to the Promised Land, God made a way by parting the river.

Friend, you can look at something and say it can't be done, or you can become creative and find a way to make it happen. No matter what you do it will be difficult, so you must find a way. You can look at the winds of adversity and say you can't do it, or you can become creative and use the wind to help you to take off. As long as you say it can't be done, it won't be done. Take the effort and create a way to make it happen. There is always a way. You are just going to have to think of a way to make it happen. The difference between the average and those who overcome average is that one creates a way to make it happen while the other has an excuse as to why it can't happen.

7. I'm just not as good as everyone else.

Another excuse many people use is that someone else is better at it than they are. That may be true, but that still doesn't mean you can't make it happen. There will always be someone else better than you, but that doesn't need to be your excuse for not doing something. There are better preachers than I, but that doesn't keep me from preaching. There are many better authors than myself, but that doesn't keep me from writing and helping people.

God knew you were the best person for the task when He showed you His will. Gideon felt there were others better than he to lead Israel, but God chose him. Saul didn't feel he was qualified to be king of Israel, but God knew he was the man for the job. The Scriptures are filled with illustrations of people who were not as good as others, but God still used them because they found a way in spite of their weaknesses.

Let me remind you that God is not as interested in your strength as He is your weakness. Paul said in 2 Corinthians 12:9, *"And he said unto me, My grace is sufficient for thee: for my strength is made perfect in weakness. Most gladly therefore will I rather glory in my infirmities, that the power of Christ may rest upon me."* The only reason you feel weak is because you are comparing yourself to others, but God tells us this is not wise. (2 Corinthians 10:12)

If you are waiting to be as good as others to step out and do something for God, then you will never overcome average. The average always does what others do. Always remember that if God called you to do something, then He will help you do it.

8. Obstacle or opportunity?

Everything you face in life will either be an obstacle or it will be an opportunity for God to do something through you. God says in 2 Chronicles 16:9, *"For the eyes of the Lord run to and fro throughout the whole earth, to shew himself strong in the behalf of them whose heart is perfect toward him. Herein thou hast done foolishly: therefore from henceforth thou shalt have wars."* God is looking for someone who simply has the belief that He can perform the great task through them if they will step out.

Everything you face in life will either be an obstacle that keeps you from doing something or an opportunity to find a way for God to do something through you. Those who overcome average are those who see opportunities in every obstacle. The obstacle doesn't need to be a roadblock; rather, let it be an opportunity to overcome average and show a world that God is powerful enough to work through you. I challenge you right now to lay your excuses down and find a way to make it happen.

9

NEVER STOP LEARNING

Every young person anticipates their graduation day. They often think that this is the last time they will ever have to open a book to study for a test. They then go off to college and realize the day of no more studying that they greatly anticipated didn't come.

They spend the next four years at college staying up late at night studying for exams. They read book after book to meet the requirements for their classes. They write essays and papers to satisfy the prerequisites of their degree. Their final year of college comes and they see the light at the end of the tunnel. The day of graduation has come, and the thought of no papers to complete, books to read or exams to take is the best thought ever. Again, they are certain they will never have to study.

The day they walk across the platform to receive their diploma comes. That diploma represents at least seventeen years of study from kindergarden to college, and for some even more. As they receive the diploma and walk into their career field, they soon learn that the learning process is never over if they want to overcome average. They quickly learn that the average never learn again and those who rise to the top spend the rest of their lives studying and learning so they can continue to achieve more.

If you want to overcome average, you are going to have to continue learning for the remainder of your life. God has given me the privilege of being around many people who've overcome average. What is amazing to me about these people is that all of them continued to study throughout life. No, they didn't go back to college to get another degree, but they studied and learned throughout life to better help those whom they served. To them, it wasn't about impressing people with how smart they were, but it was about overcoming average so they could help others become what God wanted them to be.

Some of the greatest preachers of my lifetime were men who never stopped learning. For over thirteen years of my life I was under the ministry of Dr. Jack Hyles who pastored the First Baptist Church in Hammond, Indiana. I can remember going into his office and asking him questions to which he had no answer, and he told me he would get back to me with an answer when he found it. I walked out of his office thinking I would never hear from him again on that subject only to be pleasantly surprised when he called me a week or two later to tell me the answer to my question. He went to other people who had the answer and then relayed that answer to me.

Bro. Hyles would often talk about reading books to get an idea. He often read biographies to learn from the examples of men who walked before him. He encouraged his college students to always carry a 3x5 card in their pocket to write down ideas they learned from others. Bro. Hyles never stopped learning, and that is why he overcame average.

I have had the opportunity to be around men who were multi-millionaires. What was very telling to me about these men is that they never stopped learning. They asked me questions about business when they were far more knowledgeable about business than I. These men understood that they could learn from anyone, and that is why they overcame average.

Some of the greatest Christian educators were men who never stopped learning. Just because they had several degrees behind their names didn't mean they had arrived. They understood that if they were going to continue to keep their education fresh for their students, then they had to continue to learn. This is why these educators overcame to be great educators instead of simply average ones.

It doesn't matter what field your career is in, if you are going to overcome average, then you are going have to continue the learning process throughout your life. When you stop learning, you start dying. Those who overcame average did so because they studied more than the average. The average got to a certain point in their life and determined they didn't need more knowledge. The one who overcomes average continually broadens their knowledge by learning something every day of their life. They never stop the learning process.

Proverbs 26:16 says, *"The sluggard is wiser in his own conceit than seven men that can render a reason."* One of the bad attributes of the sluggard is they always think they know more than anyone else; therefore, they stop learning. It doesn't matter what others tell them, the sluggard always knows more. The reason the sluggard never overcomes average is because they stop learning. If you are going to overcome average, you must never stop learning. Let me show you several things about the learning characteristics of those who overcome average.

1. Be teachable.

Ecclesiastes 4:13 says, *"Better is a poor and a wise child than an old and foolish king, who will no more be admonished."* This foolish king got to the point where nobody could tell him what to do. He thought he knew everything. His arrogance about what he thought he knew caused him not to be teachable.

The President of the United States will only be as great as his willingness to be advised by his cabinet members. When the president thinks he knows more than those he hired to advise him, then he is well on his way to destruction. The president surrounds himself with people who are smarter than he in their area so that he can better serve his country. If he is wise, he will learn from them so that he can better serve his country.

A person who is no longer teachable is a person who destroys themselves. A person who overcomes average will have a teachable spirit. That teachable spirit causes them to have a humility to listen to others. You have written the epitaph of your potential when people can no longer teach you. Keep a teachable spirit and you will keep your potential alive.

2. Life is a learning center.

God commands the Christian to *"Study to shew thyself approved unto God, a workman that needeth not to be ashamed, rightly dividing the word of truth."* (2 Timothy 2:15) God understood that the Christian needed to make life their learning center. The word *"study"* is an action word. In other words, the Christian is to continually study so they can *"be ready always to give an answer to every man that asketh you a reason of the hope that is in you with meekness and fear:"* (1 Peter 3:15)

Everything in life should be a lesson from which you learn. Every situation you face, battle you fight and word that is spoken should be a lesson from which you learn. Don't let moments go by in life without learning from them. There are lessons you can learn every day if you will make life a learning center. It is not about being critical of others; instead, it is about learning so that you can avoid the heartaches that others have faced.

3. You never know everything.

Proverbs 9:9 says, *"Give instruction to a wise man, and he will be yet wiser: teach a just man, and he will increase in learning."* It's interesting that the wise man receives instruction so he can be wiser. You would think that the wise man already has all the knowledge. What makes the wise man wise is that he understands he doesn't know everything.

Be willing to receive instruction in life. Don't ever develop the attitude that you know everything. The person who overcomes average is the person who realizes there is always more to learn. They realize that no matter how much knowledge they've acquired, there is still more to learn.

4. Learning is an attitude.

Elihu said in Job 34:32, *"That which I see not teach thou me: if I have done iniquity, I will do no more."* Elihu was not like Job's other three friends who were know-it-all's. His attitude was one of wanting to learn.

Be careful about being a know-it-all. Keep an attitude of learning. When you have an attitude of being willing to be taught, you will find those who can teach you are all around you. Keep the learning attitude so that you keep your potential alive.

5. Learning is a willingness to change.

When you are not willing to change, then you are not willing to learn, for learning will cause you to change what is wrong or add to what you are already doing to improve it. When you look at Job 34:32, you see that Elihu was willing to change whatever he was doing that was wrong. If he didn't have that attitude then he could not have learned.

If your mentality is, "My way or the highway," then you will never learn again. People who overcome average are not afraid to change what they are doing. If what they are doing is wrong, they will change it. They won't be so stubborn that nobody can tell them what to do. If adding something to what you are already doing will help improve it, then be willing to change. Change is only wrong when it pulls you away from Scripture. If you have to change your personality to help people, then change it. If you have to change your approach to helping people to be a better influence, then change yourself. Never be afraid of change just because it is change. Those who overcome average are willing to change when they learn something that can help them to be better.

6. Learning comes by listening.

You will never learn without listening. Proverbs 1:5 says, *"A wise man will hear, and will increase learning; and a man of understanding shall attain unto wise counsels:"* The wise man understands he must listen if he is going to learn. If he is talking all the time or ignoring those who are speaking, then he will never learn.

My mother used to say that God gave us two ears and one mouth so that we will listen twice as much as we speak. She was so right about learning to listen. Much of my education and wisdom has come from listening to others. As a youth, I was able to sit down with wise people and listen to them talk. To this day, I still enjoy being around wise people so I can learn. There are times I just sit and let them talk so I can learn. There may be one sentence or illustration they use that will teach me something invaluable for life. That will never happen if I don't listen.

Develop a listening ear. You will never learn by speaking. You learn by listening. Learn to let others talk more, and you will learn more, especially if you allow yourself to be around wise people.

7. A lack of learning causes error.

Jesus said, *"Ye do err, not knowing the scriptures, nor the power of God."* (Matthew 22:29) Why do people not know the Scriptures? Because they don't take the time to learn them. If these people had learned the Scriptures they would not have found themselves in error.

One of the biggest reasons we make mistakes is because we fail to learn. You don't make mistakes because you know something, you make mistakes because you failed to take time to learn. You can use ignorance as an excuse for making mistakes, and if you do you will continue to be average. On the other hand, if you will make life your learning center and continue to learn, then you will lessen the mistakes made and increase the potential to overcome average.

8. Reading is learning.

One of the biggest shortfalls of our day is that people don't read. With the advancement of technology, many have stopped reading. This is to their detriment and the detriment of all of society. People spend so much time using technology that they don't spend time reading.

Paul said, *"Till I come, give attendance to reading, to exhortation, to doctrine."* (1 Timothy 4:13) One of the greatest sins if Christians today is their failure to read. The phrase, *"give attendance to reading,"* is not a suggestion, it is a command. God knows that reading is part of the learning process, and that is why He commanded us to read.

You will never overcome average until you decide to continue reading. There are so many books that are filled with wisdom from which you could glean if you would only read. Don't be guilty of avoiding one of the best sources from which you can learn. If reading is a critical part of children learning, then it is surely important to your learning. It has been said, "Readers are leaders." I agree that your potential can be greatly increased if you will learn to read good books. Don't just read books for entertainment, but read books to learn.

9. Everybody is your teacher.

Proverbs 6:6 says, *"Go to the ant, thou sluggard; consider her ways, and be wise:"* The sluggard is commanded to go watch the ant. Why? Because the little ant is a teacher. I believe one of the things God is trying to show us is that everybody and everything can be your teacher if you will allow them.

Those who overcome average learn from everyone. They learn from those who follow them. One of the mistakes people make is in not learning from those whom they lead. Always remember that everyone knows something that you don't know; therefore, make it your goal to learn from them what you don't know.

Moreover, be sure to learn from history. God says, *"For whatsoever things were written aforetime were written for our learning..."* (Romans 15:4) History is filled with wisdom. If you would learn to be a student of history, you can follow their successes and avoid their failures.

Furthermore, learn from the failures of others. Don't look at failure to be critical of the person;

rather, study the circumstances of failures to learn what not to do. There are many lessons you can learn if you will study the failures of others. Those who overcome average will learn from the failures of others so they don't make the same mistake.

10. Ask questions.

I know this may seem obvious, but most people never learn because they don't ask questions. Luke 11:9 says, *"And I say unto you, Ask, and it shall be given you; seek, and ye shall find; knock, and it shall be opened unto you."* If you don't ask, you won't learn. When you have a question as to one's success in an area, don't be afraid to ask them how they achieved it. On the job training is one of the best teachers. If you ask the right questions, you will learn the right answers. If you will be a person who is not afraid to ask questions, then your life will be a continual learning center.

Those who overcome average will never stop learning. The average are those who ride off the knowledge they've learned and are not willing to learn more. Challenge yourself to learn something every day. Learning is one of the key ingredients to overcoming average.

10

TAKE ONE MORE STEP

One of my favorite classes in high school was the physical education class. Of course, it wasn't really a classroom, but it was the class that helped everyone to stay in good physical condition. You could always tell who was in shape and the ones who were out of shape by their enjoyment of the class.

One of the activities I did not enjoy in this class was running. I attended our church's private Christian school that was located in the hills of California. During track season, instead of running laps around the top of the hill, we would run down the country road that was just under one mile. I've never been a long distance person, so running that road was never easy. Making it to the end of the road was difficult, but running back was truly a test of my will. The way I made it back to the school was to continually tell myself, "Just take one more step." Every time I wanted to quit I would tell myself to take one more step.

Often, the difference between those who overcome average and the average is that those who overcome average take one more step than the average. They are not always the smartest or the most talented, they just take one more step than the average. Sometimes, they are not the best runners or the fastest runners, but they just take one more step than the average. Most of the time, the key to overcoming average is determined simply by taking one more step.

Throughout the Scriptures you find people who would not quit. One of the premiere men in the Scriptures who wouldn't quit was Joseph. Joseph endured deceit for thirty years. He always seemed to be at the wrong end of deceit. He was attacked, lied about and forgotten, yet he kept going and overcame average.

When Joseph's brothers sold him into slavery, instead of quitting he took one more step. When Potiphar's wife lied about Joseph trying to physically harm her, he didn't quit even though he was in the prison cell; instead, he just took one more step. When his fellow prisoner forgot about him being a help, instead of getting bitter Joseph took one more step. He kept on taking one more step until he became the Prime Minister of Egypt. If Joseph had not taken one more step, he would have never overcame average.

One of the things that stands out in David's list of mighty men is one man who kept taking one more step. The Philistine army attacked the Israeli troops which caused all of the men to retreat except one, Eleazar. The Scriptures tell us that he *"smote the*

Philistines until his hand was weary, and his hand clave unto the sword..." (2 Samuel 23:10)

Eleazar truly became a great man because he kept taking one more step. When the average troops around him fled, he stayed and fought the battle by taking one more step. When his hand became weary of cleaving to the sword, he kept taking one more step by swinging that sword. By taking one more step, Eleazar was able to see a great victory against the Philistines with the LORD's help. We will never know the names of the average men who retreated from the battle, but we know Eleazar was a mighty man because he took one more step. The average men fled from the battle, but it was the man who stayed and took one more step who overcame average to become a mighty man.

I'm reminded of the story of Jonathan fighting the battle alone against the Philistine army. While Saul and the rest of the army were resting beneath a pomegranate tree in Gibeah, Jonathan and his armor bearer took one more step and approached the enemy. While the average were resting, they were taking one more step. While the average tarried, they took one more step. While the average sat in the comforts of safety, Jonathan and his armor bearer took one more step and defeated the heathen armies. Jonathan and his armor bearer overcame average by taking one more step. One more step is what gave him victory. One more step is what allowed him to overcome average.

Galatians 6:9 says, *"And let us not be weary in well doing: for in due season we shall reap, if we faint not."* God reveals to us that we can easily become weary in doing right. God was truly trying to encourage the Christian to keep taking one more step. When the days come when you are weary, you must keep taking one more step so you can overcome average. This verse teaches us a few principles about taking one more step to overcome average.

1. Overcoming average is never easy.

If overcoming average were easy, then everyone would do it. God shows us that there will be times when you will become weary in doing right. He says, *"And let us not be weary in well doing..."* He didn't say that we would never get tired of doing right, but He showed us that we would become tired of doing right.

Don't think it will become easy to overcome average as a Christian. There are Christians who fill the pews of churches every Sunday who are average, but it is the army of Christians who understand the difficulty of doing right who truly overcome average and build the church.

It won't be easy to be a business person who rises above the average. If it were easy to start a business and become highly successful, then everyone would do it. The difference is that some take one more step when it's difficult and the average close the doors because it's too hard.

Pastoring a church is never going to be easy. I have young men regularly come to me and ask me to help them find a church. Many times they will tell me they want something that will pay them a full-time salary. I can understand that, but those who overcome average often take one more step and decide they will build their church and not look for a church that someone else has built. The pastor who rises above the average is the pastor who understands it will be difficult.

There is always going to be a struggle when you try to do right. You cannot let the struggle scare you away from doing right. Please understand that you will never overcome average if you are always looking for the easier way to do things. You will only overcome average by taking one more step.

2. Don't let the weariness of doing good cause you to become weary.

God says that you are not to become weary in *"well doing."* In other words, not seeing the fruit of your efforts can cause you to become weary. The reason God says not to become weary is because the fruits of doing good have not yet been seen.

If you're not careful, you will get to the point where you will wonder if it is really worth doing right because you are not seeing the fruits of your labors. Let me encourage you to take one more step and do right. It may seem as though doing right is not paying off, but you must take one more step.

When you want to start being deceitful in your business because you could make better profits, let me encourage you to take one more step and do right. When you could let up on your principles and standards of living as a Christian to be accepted by the "in crowd," let me encourage you not to become weary with your good and take one more step. There are going to be many times in your life when you are going to have to tell yourself to take one more step and do right.

3. Don't become tired of being tired.

Another thing God warns us about is being tired of being tired. In other words, you have been weary for so long that you give up because you're tired of being tired. When that time comes, you are going to have to will yourself to take one more step. You may have to grab your back leg and pick it up to help yourself take another step, and if that is what you have to do to keep going then take one more step.

Friend, constantly battling can become wearisome when you see others doing wrong and seemingly profiting. When that happens, don't allow yourself to become tired of being tired. Don't let your weariness drive you to quit. Keep taking one more step. Those who overcome average don't allow the weariness of doing right cause them to be so weary that they quit.

4. The harvest will come.

God promised, "...in due season we shall reap, if we faint not." Reaping season will come at the right time. One of our greatest problems is that we want everything to happen right now, but we must wait for the harvest to come to reap the benefits of our labors. That is why you must keep taking one more step. If you don't take one more step, you will miss the benefits of overcoming average and seeing the harvest of your labors.

Always remember that God's timing is never dependent upon our desires. God's timing is always right. God is rarely early, never late, but He is always on time. You will never reap the harvest if you don't work through the season while the harvest is ripening. There is always a planting season, growing season and harvest season. The harvest season is at the end, and the only way you will see it is by taking one more step.

Don't relax until you see the harvest. Don't loosen up while you wait on the harvest. Keep striving for the harvest with vigor by taking one more step. You will never overcome average until you learn to take one more step. Keep your intensity for right and never let up until you see the harvest has come.

Married couples who are struggling in your marriage, take one more step and do right for harvest season will come. Business person, keep taking one more step, work hard and be honest for harvest season will come. Single parent who is raising children by yourself, let me encourage you to take one more step and do right for harvest season will come. Church ministry worker, keep taking one more step of helping people for harvest season is coming. Pastor, keep taking one more step by helping your people and standing for right because harvest season is coming. Parent who is struggling to rear godly children, keep taking one more step and stick with your household rules for harvest season is coming. Christian trying to overcome a vice in your life, keep taking one more step by refusing that vice for harvest season is coming. Whatever it is with which you struggle, keep taking one more step for your harvest season will come.

After being in evangelism for about a decade, I almost quit the evangelism trail because I had not seen any fruits for my labors. I watched pastors walk their fruit across the platform and I wondered why God had not given me fruit. I came to the point where I was about to quit when God gave me an opportunity to speak on a national platform. After the service that night a young man came to me and told me that he was called to preach under my ministry several years prior to that service and was currently training at Bible college to be a pastor. It seemed within the next few months God began to show me the fruits of my labors. People would come to me and thank me for leading them to Christ. Pastors and missionaries would tell me how they were called into full-time service under my ministry or were influenced to keep going under my ministry. All this happened because I kept taking one more step. Had I quit, I would have never seen the fruits of my labors.

Friend, if you are going to overcome average, then you will have times when the only thing you can do is take one more step. Yes, thoughts of quitting may come to mind, but don't entertain those thoughts. You will become weary in doing right, but keep taking one more step and do right. Overcoming average is done by taking one more step than the average. If you are about to quit, let me encourage you to take one more step. If you will continue to take one more step, then you will eventually overcome average.

Boost your spirituality with
a daily devotional. Visit
Oldpathsjournal.com
to sign up.

11

STEPPING INTO UNDERACHIEVEMENT

The attrition rate of those who have overcome average is startling. Every year there are national scandals of people who've fallen from grace for one reason or another. Sports stars who seem to have everything in life fall from grace and never again achieve the greatness they once had. We could easily start naming the politicians who've risen to prominence only to let their actions steal their achievements.

Sadly, throughout my lifetime there have been many pastors and good church members who've succumbed to temptation. They fall from grace and try to rebuild, but they never truly get back to where they once were. At one time they seemed to have overcome average, but one action caused them to step into underachievement.

One of the things that is very frightening to me is to see how many people who are no longer in the ministry or have fallen who once had some form of influence on my life. I look at my ordination certificate and I am reminded of those who've stepped into underachievement. People who once had overcome average made a bad decision that squelched all potential. These are not bad people. In fact, these were very good people, but they made a bad decision that moved them from being a person who overcame average to an underachiever.

God says, *"And Jesus said unto him, No man, having put his hand to the plough, and looking back, is fit for the kingdom of God."* (Luke 9:62) There are several things God shows us about this person that caused them to fail. When God says, *"having put his hand to the plough,"* he is showing us that this person had the wrong mentality. This person thought that it was going to be easy to overcome average. The reason they turned back is because it wasn't easy. Overcoming average is not easy, but neither is it easy to stay above average once you get there.

Moreover, not only did they have the wrong mentality, but they were also going the wrong direction. Notice that this person was *"looking back"* instead of looking forward. You overcame average because your direction was right. Many people have quickly become underachievers because they changed directions. The direction you should be looking towards is the direction of truth. Truth must be the focus that determines all that you do.

Furthermore, this person was not properly prepared. The verse above says, *"...is not fit for the kingdom of God."* They were not only not physically prepared, but they were not mentally prepared.

Overcoming average comes by being prepared to meet the challenges you will face. You will not overcome average by living an undisciplined life. If you overcome average, you must also realize that setting the discipline aside that helped you overcome average will cause you to step into underachievement.

When you overcome average, you must realize that you will have a target on your back. Satan not only doesn't like it that you overcame average, but there will also be people who will want to destroy you. You must not let your guard down once you overcome average. You must realize that when you overcome average you will have to be more diligent about how you live so that you don't step into underachievement. As I've looked through the Scriptures and studied those who've stepped into underachievement, I find there are five things that contribute to this failure.

1. Fame

Fame has destroyed more than one person. Fame will feed a person's ego which will ultimately destroy them if they don't keep a proper estimation of themselves. Look at all the movie stars who acquired fame as a child and see where they are today. Many of them have become train wrecks in life. It is truly sad to see a young persons life, or any persons life, ruined by fame. Fame will test your character to its core, and if a person hasn't developed their character, then fame will surely destroy them.

Fame ultimately destroyed Saul. Samuel said to Saul, *"...When thou wast little in thine own sight, wast thou not made the head of the tribes of Israel, and the Lord anointed thee king over Israel?"* (1 Samuel 15:17) Before Saul ever became the king of Israel, he had a proper estimation of himself. In fact, he said about himself, *"Am not I a Benjamite, of the smallest of the tribes of Israel? and my family the least of all the families of the tribe of Benjamin? wherefore then speakest thou so to me?"* (1 Samuel 9:21) Saul didn't even think he deserved to be a king.

Yet, once he was established, his fame changed him to the point where he thought he was indestructible. Fame caused pride to set in, and that ultimately destroyed a once promising life. A man who had truly overcome average stepped into underachievement through the door of fame.

Another man who was ruined by fame was Samson. Probably, nobody in all the Scriptures had more potential than Samson. He was chosen by God before he was born. The power of God rested upon him from childhood, and he realized his power and fame.

Once Samson acquired fame, it destroyed him. He became disrespectful towards authority. He thought he could do whatever he wanted because he felt nobody could stop him. He even got to the point where he thought he was bigger than God when he said, *"...I will go out as at other times before, and shake myself. And he wist not that the Lord was departed from him."* (Judges 16:20) The fame he achieved caused him to lose all potential and step into underachievement.

Just because you've overcome average doesn't mean you have the right to do whatever you want to do. Fame has filled many people with pride. God says, *"Pride goeth before destruction, and an haughty spirit before a fall."* (Proverbs 16:18) Pride has destroyed many overachievers. Always remember that you are simply a sinner saved by the grace of God. Just because you have overcome average doesn't give you the right to do whatever you want to do. Fame does not negate the laws of sowing and reaping.

2. Fortune

The desire for money has destroyed many people who overcame average. The desire for fortune destroyed Achan. Joshua 7:20-21 says about Achan, *"And Achan answered Joshua, and said, Indeed I have sinned against the Lord God of Israel, and thus and thus have I done: When I saw among the spoils a goodly Babylonish garment, and two hundred shekels of silver, and a wedge of gold of fifty shekels weight, then I coveted them, and took them; and, behold, they are hid in the earth in the midst of my tent, and the silver under it."* Achan saw the valuable garment, the gold and silver, and that desire destroyed the victory he experienced in Jericho.

The desire of fortune also destroyed Ananias and Sapphira. When they were asked about whether they gave all to God, they lied to the Holy Spirit which resulted in their death. These two people truly could have used their wealth to help the early church, but fortune caused them to step into underachievement.

You must always keep a proper perspective concerning money. Money has changed many people. People who never had money have dramatically changed for the worse once they acquired it. You must realize that money is only a tool to help you serve the LORD.

1 Timothy 6:10 says, *"For the love of money is the root of all evil: which while some coveted after, they have erred from the faith, and pierced themselves through with many sorrows."* Notice that money of itself is not evil, but the *"love of money is the root of all evil."* Money will turn an honest business person into a crook. Money turns an honest politician into a dishonorable person who allows their vote to be bought. Money will drive good people to hurt others just to get it. You must always keep a right perspective of money. Don't let money run you, but you must run money. View money as a tool, and it won't destroy you.

3. Family

Keeping your family and marriage strong is vital to not stepping into underachievement. Solomon didn't control his marriage or family and it destroyed him. He had certainly overcome average as he was not the one who was supposed to be king. He had many older brothers who were in line to be king, but he was able to obtain the favor of God and it helped him to overcome average. Yet, his inability to control his family turned his overachievement into underachievement.

The strength of your marriage and family will highly dictate whether you will continue to enjoy the fruits of overcoming average. Many business people have lost their business because they were not able to control their family. Many pastors have lost their ministries because they didn't keep their marriage strong or nurture their family relationships. Many who overcame average stepped into underachievement because they forgot the most important relationships in their life outside of their relationship with God, and that was the relationship with their spouse and family.

You must keep your marriage strong if you are going to live above the average. Devoting time to your spouse will help you in the long run not to have to dedicate time, and energy to save your marriage or to endure the trial of divorce. When you are having problems in your marriage or family, get help before it's too late. Most people wait until the schism in their marriage or family is so large that it is too late to span it. Don't lose your family or marriage for the sake of success. You can overcome average and have a good marriage and family if you will keep everything in its proper perspective. If you will put your marriage and family before your job, then you can more easily live above the average with their support.

4. Friends

One of the areas that has ruined many success stories are the friends one acquires. One of the most prominent people in the Scriptures who let friends destroy his potential was Amnon. It is said about Amnon, *"But Amnon had a friend, whose name was Jonadab, the son of Shimeah David's brother: and Jonadab was a very subtil man."* (2 Samuel 13:3) The wrong friend led him down the wrong path, and it led him into underachieving.

You are only as strong as your weakest friend. The interesting thing about Amnon is not that he had many friends who were bad influences, but he had one friend who was a bad influence. Always remember it doesn't take many friends to influence you for wrong; it only takes one friend to influence you for wrong.

Don't ever be afraid to move away from a friend who is going the wrong direction. They are the one moving, and it is their fault that you cannot associate with them like you have before. When you live above the average, you will find many "friends" who are truly not your friend. They are only seeking you because you have done something of which they want a part. If a person didn't want any part of you before you overcame average, then be wary of them when they want to be your friend after you've overcome average.

Always determine whether you should continue to run with someone by the direction their life is going. If they are doing things you would not do, then you would be wise to distance yourself from them. Proverbs 22:3 says, *"A prudent man foreseeth the evil, and hideth himself: but the simple pass on, and are punished."* If they start choosing friends with whom you would not associate, then distance yourself from them. If they start going to places and doing things you would not do, then be a friend but not a close friend.

One of the hardest things you will have to guard to continue to live above average is in the area of friendships. Friendships have caused many people to step into underachievement. Continually re-evaluate your friendships and how close you should be so that they don't steal your success.

5. Females

I've saved this for last because this is probably one of the greatest destructions to those who have overcome average. The Book of Proverbs deals much with the subject of the strange woman. The strange woman gives great promises but delivers heartache. Proverbs 9:18 says about the end of the strange woman, *"But he knoweth not that the dead are there; and that her guests are in the depths of hell."*

Many people have destroyed promising lives and careers because of improprieties with the opposite gender. This travesty covers every walk of life. Friend, you are no different than anyone else. A one night stand with no strings attached always has strings attached.

Always be careful with the opposite gender. Never be alone with them. Always keep your private life private and never talk about it to others. Don't break down the barrier of your private life with anyone other than your spouse. You may think you are stronger than others, but it has destroyed the strongest person. Please, don't step into underachievement for the sake of the strange woman.

Friend, this chapter is written for you to beware of the dangers that will destroy you. Don't step into underachievement by allowing these areas to destroy you. Beware of them and set up guards and guidelines to keep these things from destroying the fruits of living above average.

12

Preparing the Way

What truly separates greatness from average is that greatness lives in such a manner that the next generation has no excuse to compromise. Greatness not only serves their own generation, but they also serve the next generation. They have a greater goal than just living to please themselves. They live preparing the way for those who will follow.

When you look at the forefathers of America, you see men who served their own generation and also prepared the way for generations to come. These were not average men for they were men who could see far beyond their own generation. Many of these men may have been average when they were young, but they overcame average by preparing the way for generations to come to have a nation that was free.

God prepared the way for the generations to come by giving us the Word of God. He not only gave us His Word, but He preserved His Word *"from this generation for ever."* (Psalm 12:7) God knew there were many generations to come, so He gave His Word to every generation. He inspired and preserved every word through the King James Bible so that no generation would have an excuse not to know truth.

Jesus Christ lived His life for generations to come. He not only served His own generation by starting the first church and seeing people saved, but He lived a sinless life, died on the cross and rose again so that every person in every generation would have a way to be born again. He set the ultimate example of preparing the way.

When I look at the Scriptures, I see that many of the men whom God used in a great way prepared the way for the next generation. Abraham prepared the way for Isaac when he sent his servant to find a wife for his son. Abraham said, *"The LORD God of heaven, which took me from my father's house, and from the land of my kindred, and which spake unto me, and that sware unto me, saying, Unto thy seed will I give this land; he shall send his angel before thee, and thou shalt take a wife unto my son from thence."* When you read this story, you see that Abraham didn't want Isaac to go back from whence they came, so he made sure he prepared the way for Isaac to go forward in God's will.

David prepared the way for the next generation when he set aside gold, silver and supplies for Solomon to build a temple for God. Yes, David served his own generation well, but he also lived his life so the next generation would know what life to live once he was gone. He was not so selfish as to hoard everything for himself; rather, he understood there would be someone else sitting on his throne, and that throne was given to him by God. David prepared so the next generation would know how to live for God.

Solomon learned this valuable lesson from his father, so he also prepared the way for the next generation. When you read the Book of Proverbs, you are reading the instructions of Solomon to his son. Solomon said, *"The proverbs of Solomon the son of David, king of Israel; To know wisdom and instruction; to perceive the words of understanding; To receive the instruction of wisdom, justice, and judgment, and equity; To give subtilty to the simple, to the young man knowledge and discretion."* (Proverbs 1:1-4) Solomon prepared for his son by giving him instructions in a book for him to follow. No, Solomon could not force the next generation to follow those instructions for that decision was theirs to make, but he left them with no question as to how they were to live.

Maybe the best person in the Scriptures who made no illusions about this principle was John the Baptist. Mark 1:3 says about John the Baptist, *"The voice of one crying in the wilderness, Prepare ye the way of the Lord, make his paths straight."* John's whole life was spent preparing the way for the next generation, and that next generation was Jesus Christ.

When you look at great men of God, you see men who served their own generation and the generations to come. Greatness prepares the way for the next generation to continue to do right. They understand they are only a small piece of the puzzle, and their responsibility is to be sure the next generation clearly understands their responsibility to carry on what was handed to them so they can pass it on to the next generation.

For many years I had the privilege of serving in the ministry of Dr. Jack Hyles, who pastored the First Baptist Church in Hammond, Indiana. One of the overwhelming desires of Bro. Hyles was to prepare the way for the next generation. I truly believe the reason God used him in such a great way was because he lived his life preparing for the next generation. Every decision he made had the next generation in mind. Every sermon he preached had the next generation in mind. Every action he performed had the next generation in mind. He was truly a man who showed me how to live with keeping the next generation in mind.

Those who overcome average are those who truly grasp this principle of preparing the way for the next generation. You cannot live for yourself without destroying your potential. What increases ones potential is when they realize they must live to hand to the next generation what was once handed to them.

You can equate this thought to a relay race. When I was in high school, I was the anchorman of our relay team. The starter carried a baton that was to be handed to the runner after him. Each runner was to carry the baton and hand it to the next runner until the anchorman carried the baton to the finish line. The one constant in the whole race was the baton. It started the race and it ended the race by being passed from runner to runner.

We must realize that we are one of many runners in the race of life. God says in Hebrews 12:1, *"Wherefore seeing we also are compassed about with so great a cloud of witnesses, let us lay aside every weight, and the sin which doth so easily beset us, and let us run with patience the race that is set before us,"* Every person before us ran their race handing off to each generation after them. Now, it is your responsibility to prepare the way for the generation that follows you. You will never overcome average by running for yourself. You overcome average by preparing the way for the next generation. There are five very important thoughts you must consider if you are going to prepare the way for the next generation.

1. Be careful with every decision.

Every decision you make has an impact on you and those whom you influence. Everyone has had to pay the price of another's bad decision. This is never an easy pill to swallow. Suffering because of another's poor decision making can cause others to be angry and bitter when not handled properly.

You must realize that every decision you make influences someone else. Not only will every decision influence others, it will ultimately influence the next generation. This is why you must be careful with every decision.

Proverbs 3:5-6 says, *"Trust in the Lord with all thine heart; and lean not unto thine own understanding. In all thy ways acknowledge him, and he shall direct thy paths."* Your decisions must not be based upon your feelings. They must be based upon what God would have you to do. His Word gives you clear principles in making decisions.

One of the biggest hindrances to overcoming average is poor decision making. When making a decision, never ask how it will immediately affect you; rather, how will it affect you in years to come. Furthermore, you need to be sure to make decisions based upon where the next generation will take it. Some things that we decide to do may not be bad, but the next step from that decision may be bad; therefore, you must make decisions in such a manner that the next generation will not step into sin if they move one step away from your decision.

A good illustration of this is in music. There is some music that is not bad, but it skirts an unscriptural line. If the next generation takes it one step further than your music standard, then they may take it into sin. This is why it is wise to stay more conservative on music so that the next generation won't cross over into sin.

Always take the next generation into consideration when making a decision. Always ask yourself where they will take your decision. Be sure that your decisions are not one step away from sin.

2. Your direction determines your destination.

If you want the next generation to stay strong, then you must make your spiritual direction clear. Your present stance may not be wrong, but your direction can be wrong. Many times we look at where we are standing instead of where we are looking. Where we look will determine our direction.

Psalm 1 is one of the most important passages to help with your direction in decision making. The books you read determine your direction. The people you follow determine your direction. The institutions you associate with determine your direction. You must understand that you cannot have an unclear direction and expect the next generation to go the right way. If you are going to prepare the way for the next generation, then you must make your direction clear. Make it as clear as Joshua did when he said, *"...as for me and my house, we will serve the Lord."* (Joshua 24:15)

3. Your associations must be guarded.

Your associations influence your direction. Amos 3:3 says, *"Can two walk together, except they be agreed?"* Many people have ruined the next generation by their own weak associations. If you are going to prepare the way for the next generation, you must be sure you have scriptural associations. The next generation will follow your weakest associations. If one of your associations is doing something of which the Scriptures would not approve, then you must separate from them. You may be strong enough not to let that association hurt you, but the next generation only sees them in a good light. If a friend starts going the wrong way, then be friendly at a distance, but don't run with them.

4. Your standards must be kept high.

Your personal standards must always be higher than those whom you lead. What you do in moderation the next generation will do in excess. To avoid teaching the next generation the wrong standards, keep your standards higher than what you expect from them. God always holds the leader to a higher standard. When you study the qualifications for a pastor and deacon in 1 Timothy 3, you see that God expected them to be *"blameless."* In other words, they needed to live in such a manner that no one could point their finger at them. The only way this will happen is to have a higher standard.

The next generation will normally take the standard lower than where you set it. If you want to prepare the way, you must live above the standard of others. It is not that you are better than they, it is simply that you are preparing the way for the next generation. Those who overcome average don't live like the average; they hold themselves to a higher standard.

5. You must disciple the next generation in the right ways.

You will never prepare the way until you learn to train the next generation. Deuteronomy 11:19 says, *"And ye shall teach them your children, speaking of them when thou sittest in thine house, and when thou walkest by the way, when thou liest down, and when thou risest up."* The next generation will not know how to live if you don't teach them. You don't go to them and ask them what they want to hear. You go to the Word of God and ask God what they need to be taught. Use the Word of God to teach them how to run a business properly, build a church and live the Christian life. They will never know what to carry on if you don't teach them.

Are you preparing the way for the next generation to serve the LORD? It doesn't matter if you lead one person or a thousand people, your responsibility is to be sure the next generation clearly sees the right way. Those who overcome average do so by making sure the next generation knows what they know and how to do what they do. Your greatness will not be determined by what you do in this life, but by what the next generation takes from your life. Be sure the only things they can take are the scriptural principles of right living. The best way I can end this thought is

with the famous poem, *Bridge Builder,* by Will Allen
Dromgoole.

> An old man, going a lone highway,
> Came at the evening cold and gray
> To a chasm vast and deep and wide
> Through which was flowing a swollen tide.
> The old man crossed in the twilight dim;
> The rapids held no fears for him.
> But he turned when safe on the other side
> And built a bridge to span the tide.
>
> "Old man," cried a fellow pilgrim near,
> "You're wasting your time in building here.
> Your journey will end with the closing day;
> You never again will pass this way.
> You have crossed the chasm deep and wide;
> Why build you this bridge at even-tide?"
>
> The builder lifted his old gray head.
> "Good friend, in the path I have come," he said,
> "There follows after me today
> A youth whose feet must pass this way.
> This stream, which has been as naught to me,
> To that fair youth may a pitfall be.
> He too must cross in the twilight dim —
> Good friend, I am building this bridge for him."

13

SUCCESS IS OVERRATED

One of the hottest topics that will get people's attention is success. If you go to any bookstore in your town, you will find success books all over the shelves. There is no doubt that people want to succeed, so authors feed off that desire to sell their books.

In a search for success, you will find that this topic covers many different categories. Leadership books are mainly success books written by someone who is teaching how they became a successful leader. There are scores of real estate books being sold to show the reader how they can succeed in the real estate market if they will follow a particular model. The financial market is filled with success books showing the reader how to invest so they can become financially successful.

The problem with success is that it is relative. In other words, what one considers success may be considered a failure by another. Success is usually measured in relation or in proportion to something or someone else. We usually measure success by whether we have more than someone else which is truly a poor measurement of success.

Success is very overrated. We make success sound as if it can be guaranteed, but the truth is no one can ever guarantee success. In fact, the word "success" is used only one time in the Scriptures and it is in reference to living a godly life. Joshua 1:8 says, *"This book of the law shall not depart out of thy mouth; but thou shalt meditate therein day and night, that thou mayest observe to do according to all that is written therein: for then thou shalt make thy way prosperous, and then thou shalt have good success."* God says success is the result of living according to the Word of God.

My favorite college football team is the University of Alabama. Let me say to all my fellow fans, "Roll Tide!" I have been an Alabama fan since I was a child. I love watching their games and truly cherish their winning history.

The second winningest coach when it comes to national championships in Alabama history is Nick Saban. Coach Saban did not develop a winning team by guaranteeing the players that they could win. Instead, he built a program by setting standards by which the players should play. He tells the players that he cannot guarantee a win, but if they will play to the standard of their program that they will place themselves in the best situation to win. Instead of playing to win, they play to a standard. That has resulted in a winning program and several championships. It has built what many would call a successful program.

Living to a standard is what God wants for His people. Instead of encouraging Christians to strive for success, you will find that God sets standards by which He expects His children to live. The good thing about living to a standard is that anyone can do it and succeed. One's intellect doesn't determine whether one can live to God's standard. A person who is intellectually challenged and the person of intellectual strength can both live to God's standard.

When one chooses to live to a standard, then ones physical makeup doesn't hinder achievement. The one who sits in a wheelchair or who is physically impaired can live to God's standard. Likewise, the one who is physically strong and healthy can live to the same standard as those who are physically impaired. Living to a standard can be achieved by both.

Living to a standard is not determined by ones background. The person who grew up on the other side of the tracks can live to the same standard as the one who grew up in a wealthy community. The one who grew up in a broken or dysfunctional home can live to the same standard as the one who grew up in a tight knit family with both parent's support. One's background does not determine whether one can live to a standard because no matter what your background may be, you can live to a standard.

Living to a standard cannot be a choice or a suggestion; rather, it must be a requirement. The

Christian who wants to produce fruit must live by a standard. The ministry that wants to reach their world and create a fruit-bearing ministry must live to a standard. The business that desires to build a profitable portfolio year in and year out must work and produce to a standard. Living to a standard in any field can be achieved by all who are involved, and anything short of the standard cannot be acceptable.

God wants His children to live to a standard instead of living to succeed. If you will live to a standard, then you will give yourself the best chance of "succeeding" in life. Don't let success intimidate you; instead, live to God's standard and success will find you. The individual, business person, ministry leader or person in any specialized field can benefit from living to God's standard. There are six standards to which God expects us to live.

1. Holiness

Leviticus 19:2 says, *"Speak unto all the congregation of the children of Israel, and say unto them, Ye shall be holy: for I the Lord your God am holy."* God's requirement for the Christian is not to live up or down to another's lifestyle, but to be holy. In other words, make Christ your standard of living.

We live in times when many move the standard of holiness according to the present culture. That doesn't produce a good Christian. To reach our potential for Christ, we must live according to God's standard of holiness. God's Word is filled with the standards of holiness. God did not set these standards because He wanted His children to be miserable; rather, He set these standards of holiness because He knows what is best for our lives.

For instance, every vehicle that you purchase has an owner's manual. That manual tells you how to take care of the car so you can get the most out of it. It tells you how often to change the oil and rotate the tires so the engine and tires will last longer. Those rules are not in the manual to inconvenience the owner; rather, they are in there so the owner can get the most enjoyment and usefulness out of their vehicle.

God's standard of holiness is set so that any person can get the most enjoyment out of their life. God knows what is best for every person because He made us; therefore, God's standard of holiness is set by the Word of God. It does not change! God's standard of holiness says that drinking alcohol is wrong because He knows what it will do to a family and the life of the individual who drink it. God's standard of holiness says that adultery and fornication are wrong. God is not trying to make you miserable; instead, He is trying to keep you healthy and help you to avoid the diseases and heartache that a promiscuous life brings.

These are just a couple of God's standards of holiness. Holiness must be the expectation. Anything less than God's holiness in our life will cause us not to achieve the potential that God intended for us to achieve.

2. Excellence

Excellence is a choice. You choose to expect excellence or you choose mediocrity. Excellence is simply doing your best and not expecting anything less. God says, *"And whatsoever ye do, do it heartily, as to the Lord, and not unto men;"* (Colossians 3:23) God wants everything that you do to be done to the best of your ability.

When I was a boy, my mother instilled in me the expectation of excellence. When she gave me a job to do, she would always come back and inspect it when I was done. When she told me to dust my room, she would come in when I was done and see if I did a good job. Whenever she found that I dusted around the objects on my furniture, she lifted them up and told me that I wasn't finished. She used to say, "If it's worth doing, then do it right the first time."

With whatever you do, don't accept second-rate quality. Expect excellence! James 4:17 says, *"Therefore to him that knoweth to do good, and doeth it not, to him it is sin."* We serve a God of excellence, and anything short of excellence is sin. When doing a project, expect excellence. Don't ever say, "Well, that will do." No, it won't! Excellence is to be expected and achieved by all.

3. Effort

God wants us to give our best effort in all that we do. He says in Mark 12:30, *"And thou shalt love the Lord thy God with all thy heart, and with all thy soul, and with all thy mind, and with all thy strength: this is the first commandment."* Notice, God did not measure your strength by another's, but He wants you to give all of your strength.

What I love about this is that no matter what your strength level is, you can give it all. If your strength wains because of health, you can still give your full effort. If you are healthy and have strength that endures for a long time, you can still give your full effort. God's standard of full effort can be achieved by all because it is simply measured according to your individual strength.

Never give a half-hearted effort in anything that you do. The standard by which you should live is to give all of your strength to anything you put your hand to do. Don't ever start something when you are not going to give your full effort.

4. Obedience

Obedience is doing what you are told to do when you don't want to do it. The opposite of obedience is rebellion. God told Saul, *"...to obey is better than* sacrifice, and to hearken than the fat of rams." (1 Samuel 15:22) Saul thought he could justify his disobedience and rebellion by giving a spiritual excuse, but God made it clear that His standard is obedience.

Anybody can obey God. Obedience is not a skill, but a choice and an action. God says, "For rebellion is as the sin of witchcraft..." (1 Samuel 15:23) Obedience to the rules and orders of authority is not to be a choice; it is to be expected. You will never excel in life until you learn to obey those who are over you. The greatest leaders are the greatest followers. Jesus Christ lived to the standard of obedience by obeying His Father.

Obedience to God's Word is the standard by which you should live. Don't pick and choose what you want to obey, for that is disobedience. Obey all of God's Word, for that is the standard by which God expects you to live.

5. Sanctification

Sanctification is simply continually growing into the image of God. God expects continual growth. He says in Leviticus 20:7, "Sanctify yourselves therefore, and be ye holy: for I am the Lord your God." The word "sanctify" means a continual setting apart or cleaning. In other words, God standard is for us to be continually growing.

2 Peter 3:18 says, *"But grow in grace, and in the knowledge of our Lord and Saviour Jesus Christ. To him be glory both now and for ever. Amen."* Notice, God doesn't say how much to grow, it is simply a command to grow. Notice again, God doesn't say grow to a certain level and then stop; He simply says to grow. In other words, you are to grow, and grow and continue growing until the day you die.

Continual improvement must always be the standard that you expect. The status quo must never be accepted. Just because you are as good as someone else does not mean that is good enough. Any organization must expect continual improvement from its employees, volunteers and management if they want to excel. A Christian must never stop trying to grow in Christ. Always remember there is room for improvement no matter how good you are.

6. Dedication

Dedication is a commitment to Christ. Matthew 6:33 says, *"But seek ye first the kingdom of God, and his righteousness; and all these things shall be added unto you."* God wants the Christian to dedicate their life to Him. Anything that would pull the Christian away from Christ must not be done. Even if what would pull you away is not bad, it becomes bad when it affects your dedication to Christ.

Let's say a person decides to invest in purchasing real estate. Purchasing real estate is not bad. In fact, it is often a very good investment. Purchasing real estate is not bad in and of itself, but when it pulls the Christian away from serving the LORD, then purchasing real estate becomes wrong. God wants total dedication to His will for your life.

I don't know what God's will is for your life. Maybe God's will is to be a business person or to work in a factory. Maybe God's will is to work in an office or in the financial world. Maybe God's will is to be a pastor, evangelist or missionary. Whatever God's will is for your life, you must be dedicated to what He made you to do. Remember that your field of employment always comes second to your dedication to God. If a better paying job or a higher position would take you away from serving God, then you must not take it. A total dedication to God is the standard by which you must live.

Those who overcome average live to a standard. They don't strive to succeed; they strive to live according to God's standard. The average think these things are a choice or a suggestion, but those who overcome average understand these standards for living are expected and must not be ignored. Overcoming average in your life will be highly determined by whether you live to a standard; the standard of God.

14

TRUTH DRIVEN

Years ago I was taking a flight from Salinas, California to Albuquerque, New Mexico. My father, two teenage young men and I were flying to a church planting conference in New Mexico. Because I had my pilots license, we thought it would be cheaper if I flew us all to the conference.

We stopped in Needles, California to refuel the plane. After taking off from Needles, we were about midway through this leg of the trip when we encountered a monsoon storm in Arizona. I looked all around me and dark clouds had literally surrounded the plane as if they were about ready to attack. I looked at my map and quickly realized that the only airports where I could land were on the other side of the storm.

With this realization, I called to Albuquerque tower to see if they could vector me around the storm to the nearest airport. They radioed back to me that there was no airport and that I would have to fly through the storm. They set my heading to what they thought was the weakest part of the storm. I looked at what was straight ahead of me and I knew we were in for the ride of our lives.

As I approached the wall of the storm, I could see lightening all around. Right before I entered the storm, the tower notified me that they would not be able to see me on radar, but we could still communicate via radio. The electrical storm would keep the tower from seeing me. With a prayer under my breath and tightening my grip on the yoke, we entered the storm.

As I expected, this storm produced a rough ride. The four passenger seat airplane that we were flying in was being tossed around in the storm like a child hitting a piñata. The first thing that came to my mind while I was flying through the storm was the training I had received from my instructor. He drilled inside of me that if I ever found myself in the clouds or in a storm, I was to keep my eyes on the instruments of the airplane. He told me that my instruments were my bible in the sky. That advice got me through the storm. Though lightening was flashing in front of the propeller and at the edges of the wings, I kept flying by my instruments so I could safely make my way through the storm.

Those instruments were my source of truth. The instruments kept me on course even in the most violent storm I had ever flown through. If I had flown by the seat of my pants, I could have likely found myself on the side of a mountain because we could not see where we were going. Those instruments in that plane were truly my bible in the sky. They were the truth that drove me and guided me through the storm.

If you are going to overcome average, then truth must be the fire that stirs your soul. It was truth that drove Jeremiah. Notice what he says in Jeremiah 20:9, *"Then I said, I will not make mention of him, nor speak any more in his name. But his word was in mine heart as a burning fire shut up in my bones, and I was weary with forbearing, and I could not stay."* It bothered Nehemiah that people would not defend truth. When he got discouraged, the desire for truth still burnt inside of him and drove him to keep going. Being driven by truth is what caused Jeremiah to overcome average.

It was truth that drove a young David to be willing to face Goliath. When he heard Goliath cursing his God, he volunteered to risk his life to fight this giant. When others came to him and told him he was going too far, he said to them, *"...What have I now done? Is there not a cause?"* (1 Samuel 17:29) What caused David to overcome average was that he was driven by truth. He could not sit idly by and watch truth be attacked and maligned. It lit a fire in his heart that caused him to do something he normally would not have done.

Being truth driven is what caused Shadrach, Meshach and Abednego to be willing to go into the fiery furnace instead of bowing down to the golden image. They said in Daniel 3:17-18, *"If it be so, our God whom we serve is able to deliver us from the burning fiery furnace, and he will deliver us out of thine hand, O king. But if not, be it known unto thee,*

O king, that we will not serve thy gods, nor worship the golden image which thou hast set up." It didn't matter to them if they won or lost, they were not going to allow truth to be defeated. It was that fire for the proclamation of truth that drove them to stand and face the fiery furnace rather than compromise with the rest of the crowd.

Those who overcome average are people who understand that they must stay focused on truth. One of the greatest problems we face today is there seems to be a lack of love for truth. What I mean is that very few people today want truth more than anything else. If truth is covered, many don't care as long as it doesn't inconvenience them. You will never overcome average with this mentality. There are several characteristics of those who overcome average and their attitude towards truth.

1. Those who overcome average believe in absolutes.

One of the causes of people being average is that they have no absolutes. They believe that truth changes over time depending upon a culture or ones conscience; whereas, those who overcome average believe truth is absolute. The belief that there is an absolute is what motivates those who overcome average to spread truth. Being a person who has absolutes takes backbone, and that is why those are the ones who will stand when others change right along with society. Believing in absolutes is what causes those who overcome average to put their life, finances and everything on the line for the sake of spreading and defending truth. Without absolutes, they would never sacrifice these things.

2. Everything is either right or wrong.

You will never overcome average until you believe there is always a right way and a wrong way; there can be no gray areas. To understand this you must realize that Jesus Christ is truth. John 14:6 says, *"Jesus saith unto him, I am the way, the truth, and the life: no man cometh unto the Father, but by me."* We are then told that Jesus never changes in Hebrews 13:8, *"Jesus Christ the same yesterday, and to day, and for ever."* So, if Jesus never changes, and Jesus is truth, then everything is either right or wrong.

One plus one equals two no matter how you do it. There is no middle ground or gray area to this equation. Likewise, there are no gray areas in life. Every decision you make is either right or wrong.

In the Book of Judges we are told, *"...every man did that which was right in his own eyes."* (Judges 21:25) The result of this was total chaos and a falling away from truth. They hurt their potential because they would not identify truth.

Understanding there is a right and a wrong in everything you do is what determines whether you stay average or overcome average. Overcoming average is partly achieved by understanding the rights and wrongs of everything you do. This acknowledgement of truth is what will drive you to keep going until you overcome average.

3. Truth must be the horizon that drives any cause.

Proverbs 3:3 says, *"Let not mercy and truth forsake thee: bind them about thy neck; write them upon the table of thine heart:"* Truth should always come first, then the cause comes after truth. You will notice that God gave His Word, then He gave the cause to reach the world with the Gospel. There is no Gospel without God's Word which is the source of all truth.

Just like I had to keep my eyes on the instruments in that airplane, you must keep your eyes on truth as you pursue a cause. Whatever your cause is, truth must be the driving force behind it.

The cause of freedom that drove our forefathers came from the truth that God gave every person a free choice. The truth that every man was created equal is what gave the cause to write the Declaration of Independence. Causes that are driven by truth are worthy and life changing causes.

4. Causes must not drive truth.

This is the complete opposite of the previous point. Many get let their cause determine truth which leads to compromise. Many good people have changed because they have allowed their cause to determine their truth. When the cause of seeing the world saved overrides truth, then you will change truth to see anyone saved.

Jude 1:3 says, *"...earnestly contend for the faith..."* God didn't say to contend for a cause, but for the faith. The faith is truth. You must be careful not to let your burden for a cause blind you from the truth for which you are to contend.

5. When a cause disagrees with truth, then the cause is wrong.

Causes can be noble, but if they disagree with truth then they are wrong. It doesn't matter how the cause is painted, truth determines whether the cause is right or wrong. A cause may seem compassionate, but if it does not agree with truth then it is wrong. Causes will stir feelings and emotions, but just because it feels right or emotionally moves someone doesn't make it right. Truth always dictates whether a cause is right or wrong.

6. The end must not justify the means.

Herein is where many fall away. Many look at results instead of truth, and they change what they think is hindering them from getting their results, even if it means they must sacrifice truth to get what they want. Many pastors want to have a large church because they feel it will help them to be more influential in their community. The end doesn't justify the means even if it does give you more influence. Truth is the only thing that justifies the means. If truth must be "changed" to accommodate getting the result desired, then don't do it.

7. Your closeness to God is determined by your love for truth.

Your love for truth ultimately determines how close you get to God. Psalm 145:18 says, *"The Lord is nigh unto all them that call upon him, to all that call upon him in truth."* If you are not driven by truth, then you cannot be close to God, for God is truth. He is the only One Who helps you overcome average. The cause of truth must drive you, for without it you will never access the power of God to enable you to overcome average. The average stay near man, but those who overcome average in the Christian life are always near God. If you desire to be close to God, then become truth driven.

15

Tried, Tested and Proven to Work

One of the main ingredients of those who overcome average is that principles direct their decisions. They have learned that making a decision based upon principle is one of the safest ways to avoid disaster. They know that principled decisions have been tested, so they are willing to stake their future on that which has already been tested.

When David was about ready to face Goliath, Saul called him in to interview him. Saul asked David what kind of fighting experience he had. David responded by telling him of two different situations he faced when watching his father's sheep in the field. He told Saul that while he was watching his father's sheep, a lion came into the field and took a lamb from the flock. He said he went after the lion and killed it. Then not long after that instance, a bear came and took another lamb from the flock. David quickly went after the bear and killed the bear with his hands and saved the lamb. He said, "...*The Lord that delivered me out of the paw of the lion, and out of the paw of the bear, he will deliver me out of the hand of this Philistine...*" (1 Samuel 17:37) This was certainly a great resumé for David to use in fighting Goliath, the champion of the Philistines. One would think that a lion and bear would be much greater opponents than this Philistine giant.

Saul then asked David if he had any armor. David told Saul that he had never fought with armor, so he didn't have any. Saul then compelled David to use his armor. After trying on Saul's armor David said, *"I cannot go with these; for I have not proved them."* (1 Samuel 17:39) What David was saying was that he needed something that had already been tried, tested and proven to work. He didn't want to go to battle with unproven armor.

This is very much the epitome of living by principle. Just like David wanted to go to battle with what had been tried, tested and proven to work, you must make decisions based upon principles that have been tried, tested and proven to work. One of the reasons there are so few people who overcome average is because there are very few people who truly live by principle. Those who live by principle find that it's not very difficult to overcome average. It's not difficult because you are simply copying that which has been tried, tested and proven to work.

WHAT IS A PRINCIPLE?

A principle is a fundamental truth that is the foundation of decision making. The principle is where you go to make your decisions. It is the guiding instrument to which you look to help make decisions.

Just like a mechanic goes to a maintenance book to find the specs on calibrating parts of a car, a person who lives by principles will run to their principles to determine what decisions to make.

Principles are predetermined decisions. In other words, a principle has been determined before the pressure of the decision is upon you. Let me illustrate. When I took flying lessons, they taught us what to do if our plane went into a spin. They drilled that into us over and over again. One day when I was practicing some maneuvers, I accidentally went into a spin. Immediately, my mind when to the lessons I learned on recovering from a spin and I followed those instructions. That saved me from hurting myself and maybe even losing my life. Knowing what you will do before you are faced with something takes all the pressure off making decisions.

Furthermore, living by principle comes from having a purposed heart. When Daniel was faced with eating the king's meat, he didn't have to think about what he was going to do because he had already purposed in his heart what he would do. Daniel 1:8 says, *"But Daniel purposed in his heart that he would not defile himself with the portion of the king's meat, nor with the wine which he drank: therefore he requested of the prince of the eunuchs that he might not defile himself."* This was not a spur of the moment decision, this was a principled decision that came from a purposed heart.

If you don't have a purpose in your heart to do something, then you will find it hard to make principles by which to live. Having a purposed heart to serve God without compromise will guide you to scriptural principles. Without a purposed heart, you have no guide to help you in setting up your principles. Principles come from the purpose you set in your heart.

HOW TO DEVELOP PRINCIPLES

How you develop your principles is as important as having them. A person without principles will not overcome average. Likewise, a person who doesn't properly develop principles will also not overcome average. Properly developing your principles is the key to having something that has been tried, tested and proven to work.

The first place you go to develop your principles is the Word of God. This should be a given. 2 Timothy 3:16-17 says, *"All scripture is given by inspiration of God, and is profitable for doctrine, for reproof, for correction, for instruction in righteousness: That the man of God may be perfect, throughly furnished unto all good works."* God's Word is the foundation for all decisions. God's Word shows you the right and wrong of what to do. When God's Word tells you something is right or wrong, then that has set the principle by which you make decisions concerning those things. Following God's Word is a sure way to make certain you have principles that have been tried, tested and proven to work.

The second place you go to develop your principles is history. Look at history and ask yourself, "What has history taught me about what I need to do in every circumstance." One of the greatest things we learn from history is that we don't learn from history. It is foolish to think that you are different from those in the past. If history shows that something is successful, then you will be successful if you do the same thing. If history shows that something causes failure, then you will fail if you follow the same path. History is a great place to develop your principles because the principles of the past have been tried, tested and proven to work.

The third place you go to develop your principles is your own personal experiences. What has your experience taught you? Oftentimes you can answer your questions of what you ought to do by looking at your own experience. Don't try to reinvent the wheel. If something has worked, just keep doing it over and over again. Your personal experience is critical to developing principles that have been tried, tested and proven to work.

WHAT IS THE IMPORTANCE OF PRINCIPLES?

Principles are a very important part of keeping your life stable. It can never be stressed enough the importance of principles in making good decisions.

Oftentimes decisions impact your life for a lifetime. If they are that important, then having principles to guide you is critical to your future.

Principles also take the feelings and emotions out of decision making. One of the greatest contributors to poor decision making is our feelings and emotions. Just because something may feel right doesn't make it right. I often tell people that if you want a feeling then stick your finger in a light socket and turn it on. You will most certainly get a feeling, but that is not good for your health.

Feelings are based off the emotion of the moment. Emotions are not a stable indicator of what you should do. If times are good, then emotions will be riding high, but if times are bad then your emotions will cause you to shy away from something that could be helpful to you. Principles take the emotions and feelings out of the decision because they were previously set.

For instance, using principles to purchase a vehicle would be wise. When you get around a new car, your feelings and emotions get involved. Your feelings and emotions tell you to figure out a way to purchase that new car. On the other hand, your principles will slow you down and cause you to go through the numbers of what the car costs and compare that to your monthly budget. Your principles in many cases will keep you from financial disaster in this area because they remove your feelings and emotions.

Principles will also help you to decide your loyalties. When you live by principles, your loyalty to God and His Word become preeminent. Thus, your principles will keep you from placing your loyalties in personalities and institutions. When personalities and institutions go astray, your principles will tell you where you need to stand.

Furthermore, principles allow you to make less decisions. When you have to make fewer decisions, then you have a better chance of avoiding bad decisions. Principles were made before you were faced with the decision; therefore, it keeps you from having to make multiple decisions. When you run to your principles every time a decision must be made, often the principle will make the decisions for you.

Moreover, principles have a higher success rate. They have a higher success rate because they are based off that which has been tried, tested and proven to work. It is highly unlikely that a principle will lead you down the wrong path.

WHAT ARE SOME IMPORTANT SITUATIONAL PRINCIPLES TO HAVE?

There are going to be many situations in which you will have to make decisions. These situations rarely change. The following are some of my situational principles that have helped me in decision making and in life.

1. Never allow money to be an issue in your ministry.

When money becomes more important than the people you are serving, then you will base decisions off how much money you will lose or gain by an action. Money must not come into the equation when making spiritual decisions.

2. Don't use your people to build your work, but use your work to build your people.

It is vitally important that no matter what you do in life, you do it to build people. Take selfishness out of your decision making. Make your life about building people instead of using people to build you.

3. Never be alone with the opposite sex.

I don't know how much I can stress this, but please follow this principle. Many people have ruined their marriages, careers and given ammunition to the enemies of Christ by being immoral. If you are never alone with the opposite sex, you will never be immoral.

4. Always be a friend to your friends.

You only have one life to live. Be friendly to your friends and be a friend to them. You will get old some day, and if you run off all your friends, you will find yourself a lonely person.

5. Never make a purchase when you do not know how you will pay it back.

Purchasing something should not be a gamble. If you know how you can pay something back before you purchase it, then you have taken unnecessary financial pressure off your life.

6. Never make a decision when you are discouraged.

Discouragement breaks your decision maker. When you find yourself in a moment of discouragement, delay the decision until your decision maker is fixed.

7. Always do for one what you would do for another.

The best way to keep heartache away from your life is to treat everyone the same. The Scriptures talk much about being just with people. If you treat everyone the same, then you will most likely not be accused of being preferential or prejudiced.

8. Never base your decisions on personalities or institutions.

Personalities and institutions regularly change. Financial pressures will cause institutions to change their beliefs. Personalities often change because life's situations change. Let your principles be based off the Scriptures, history, and personal experience because those things have already happened and will not change. Loyalties to personalties and institutions have caused many to make foolish decisions. There is only One to Whom you should be loyal and that is Christ.

9. Give your spouse veto power in your marriage.

If you are going to have a successful marriage, then your spouse needs to have veto power in your decisions. If your spouse doesn't approve of a purchase, then wait until you've shown that it is a good decision and you are both in agreement. If your spouse says you shouldn't talk to someone of the opposite gender, listen. They know their own gender better than you, and they better know and understand their intentions.

Let me conclude this chapter by saying that your principles need to be written down. You will forget your principles if you don't have them written down. Having them on paper will help you to evaluate each decision in your life.

Moreover, don't inflict your principles on others and become intolerant. In other words, don't expect others to live by your principles. These principles are yours and not theirs. You are not the spiritual policeman, so let God deal with others regarding their principles.

Overcoming average does not happen by mistake. Principles truly are the key tool to overcoming average. Without them, you continue to be average. With them, you will find yourself avoiding the pitfalls that keep you from overcoming average.

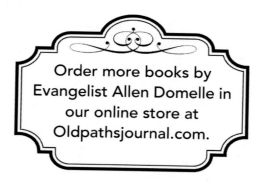

Order more books by
Evangelist Allen Domelle in
our online store at
Oldpathsjournal.com.

16

Forward Thinking

Dealing with opportunities that come your way will make or break your possibility of overcoming average. Those who overcome average have acquired a thinking process that is different from most. Instead of making a decision based upon what an opportunity will do for them, they make decisions based upon a forward direction.

A man of God came to ask my advice about what he should do with his life. This man of God was not a novice, and God was using him in a great way; however, this man of God knew that he needed to move on from what he was currently doing for God. He knew that God's will was for him to leave a position at a church to go pastor.

This man of God was not running from God, and truly had proven himself worthy of becoming a pastor. He was not running from a bad situation. He was not trying to use the call of God as his option to get away. He truly believed that it was God's will for his life to go pastor.

What he struggled with was when he should leave and which opportunity of the pastorate to take. As he and I talked about his future, I told him the one thing that must always be a part of his decision making was the direction of the decision. I told him the decision he made should never be a lateral move. This man of God had other opportunities that would have been good opportunities for most, but they were lateral moves for him. I told him that every decision he made should be with a forward direction.

Those who overcome average will not make lateral moves in life, because lateral moves are unproductive. Lateral moves take no faith and have no challenge. On the other hand, a forward move always creates a challenge and takes faith to accomplish. This is what separates those who are average from those who overcome average.

The children of Israel made the mistake of wanting to make a lateral move, and they paid for that decision with forty years of wandering. I truly believe that the reason God was so upset with Israel over not going into the Promised Land was because they chose not to move forward. God's direction is always forward, and they chose to move sideways.

When the children of Israel left the land of Egypt, they found themselves trapped between the Red Sea and the Egyptian army. God told Moses, *"...Wherefore criest thou unto me? speak unto the children of Israel, that they go forward:"* (Exodus 14:15) God did not want the children of Israel to move sideways or backwards because that was a sign of a lack of faith. God's command was to move forward.

The direction God wanted His people to take throughout the Scriptures was always forward. Forward thinking requires faith in God. Forward thinking requires hard work. Forward thinking is a challenge. Moving laterally was more about maintaining instead of conquering, and God wants His children to conquer.

We live in times when many people are more concerned with the opportunity of a decision than they are about the direction it takes them. Many are looking for the bigger and better position so that they can acquire status and be recognized. Pastors are looking for the bigger church instead of looking for the church that will take them forward. They want the work that gives them instant notoriety so they can travel and have the benefits, but they lose the forward motion and begin a lateral motion to maintain.

You will find that the mindset of those who overcome average is to move forward. They love the challenge and the faith it takes to make this move. Every Christian should set their mindset to always move forward. They should live in a forward motion and not a lateral or backwards motion. You should never be satisfied with maintaining. Your decisions should always take you forward because the will of God is always a forward motion.

There are two things that are characteristic of forward thinking. First, forward thinking always takes more faith. Hebrews 11:6 says, *"But without faith it is impossible to please him: for he that cometh to God must believe that he is, and that he is a rewarder of them that diligently seek him."* Faith is the core of forward thinking.

Business leaders who overcome average have more faith than the average businessman. That is what makes them forward thinkers and causes them to branch out into greater endeavors. The forward thinking separates the average business leader from those who overcome average.

The preacher who lives by faith and always chooses to move forward will always take steps that try their faith. Paul said concerning the church in Thessalonica, *"We are bound to thank God always for you, brethren, as it is meet, because that your faith groweth exceedingly, and the charity of every one of you all toward each other aboundeth;"* (2 Thessalonians 1:3) Notice that the forward thinking of this church caused them to grow their faith. The preacher who is willing to make decisions that require more faith will always be the preacher who is willing to put God to the test to see if He will come through on His promise to always be there for you when stepping out by faith.

Some of the forward thinkers in the Scriptures were people who were not afraid to take greater risks of faith. Abraham was a forward thinker who would not allow his son to return from where they came. Joshua and Caleb were forward thinkers who were not afraid to test their faith in God and go forward to conquer the Promised Land. Elijah was a forward thinker who had challenged his faith in God to send fire from Heaven and consume an altar. If you are going to become a forward thinker, then you must be willing to take opportunities that require more faith.

The second characteristic of forward thinking is that they are willing to accept greater challenges. They don't move because it is a better opportunity, but they move because it creates a greater challenge than their current situation. Sometimes forward thinking can look like a backwards move, but it is truly a forward move because it challenges a person to do more by going forward.

We must stop moving because an opportunity is a way to work our way up the ladder. If your move is forward, then it will create a greater challenge and may not always give you greater status. Why was the Promised Land a forward move? It was a forward move because of the challenge to overcome the massive walls, the great giants and the iron chariots. What a challenge!

Forward thinkers love greater challenges. It drives them to see how they can take what they are doing to greater heights. It can sometimes be a pastor moving from a larger church to a smaller church, but the smaller church creates a greater challenge to build with God's help. Yes, the greater challenge also takes more faith. It takes faith because you believe this opportunity is what God wants you to do, even though it challenges you.

Forward thinking is not about you getting recognition, but it is about God getting the glory. The whole reason God brought Israel out of Egypt was so that He would get the glory. Forward thinking truly allows God to get the glory. He gets the glory because He was the One Who had to help you when you accepted the opportunity which required more faith.

You will never overcome average until you acquire a mindset of forward thinking. Lateral thinking always takes less faith and a sense of maintaining. It is critical that you change your mindset from that of a lateral thinker to a forward thinker so that you can overcome average.

17

The Humility of Overachievers

Confidence can many times be mistaken for arrogance. Overachievers are oftentimes mistakenly described as cocky, when in reality they are simply confident. When you get to personally know the overachiever, you will often find them to be very humble.

Their confidence being mistaken for pride comes from the overachiever knowing what they are doing and where they are going. They usually take charge and believe that their way is the best way. This sometimes causes the underachiever to perceive the overachiever as arrogant because they take charge of a situation. If you know what you are doing, you can't help but take charge of a situation. Somebody has to take charge, and usually that is when an overachiever is discovered.

Humility is always found in those who overcome average. They know from whence they came, and many times never forget their humble beginnings. This humility of those who overcome average is not a show, neither is it a parade of an attitude that tries to prove they are humble. Instead, you will find that those who overcome average are truly humble people. They are real and very transparent, and many times are amazed that God would use them in a powerful way. The Scriptures are filled with people who overcame average, and in each instance you will find them exhibiting humility.

When the Midianites invaded the land of Israel, God sent a prophet to call Gideon to deliver them. It is interesting that God tells his background as coming from the tribe of Manasseh and from a poor family. He called himself the least of his family, yet God still called him. When Gideon was approached about being the deliverer of Israel he said, "...*Oh my Lord, wherewith shall I save Israel? behold, my family is poor in Manasseh, and I am the least in my father's house.*" (Judges 6:15) He didn't see himself as worthy to be the leader; instead, he felt others were more qualified than he. It was this humble spirit that God liked, and that is what enabled him to overcome average and become the great leader.

When David was anointed to be king of Israel, you see that he was not the first choice of anyone but God. When Samuel went to Jesse's house to anoint one of his sons to be king, he looked at all of them and God didn't accept any of them. Yet, when Samuel came to David, he didn't believe David could be king. God reminded Samuel, "...*Look not on his countenance, or on the height of his stature; because I have refused him: for the Lord seeth not as man seeth; for man looketh on the outward appearance, but the Lord looketh on the heart.*" (1 Samuel 16:7)

God looked at the heart of David and saw a humble young man who was simply honored to be used by God.

When God called Moses to lead Israel, Moses kept on trying to find a way to get out of leading Israel because he didn't feel like he was worthy. He said to God, "...*Who am I, that I should go unto Pharaoh, and that I should bring forth the children of Israel out of Egypt?...*" (Exodus 3:11) Moses was not filled with pride as one who felt he deserved to be the leader; rather, he was trying to convince God that there were others who were more qualified than he. You can see Moses' humility when God said, "*(Now the man Moses was very meek, above all the men which were upon the face of the earth.)*" (Numbers 12:3)

Consider the humility of some of the other great leaders in the Scriptures. Saul hid in the bush when Samuel was showing the people who should be the first king of Israel. He wanted no part of being the leader. Nehemiah was a waiter for the king. He had a burden for his hometown, and the only reason he stepped up was because no one else would do it. Joseph was the hated brother to whom nobody would listen. Yet, his humility allowed Pharaoh to promote him to Prime Minister of Egypt.

Every person whom God uses in a mighty way will always be found to be humble. Humility is more than an attitude, it is having a proper perspective of ones self and never forgetting it no matter how great they become. God always uses the humble. James 4:6 says, *"But he giveth more grace. Wherefore he saith, God resisteth the proud, but giveth grace unto the humble."* Those who overcome average will always have a humble spirit, and are honored that God would even use them. Let me give you several observations about the humility of those who overcome average.

1. None of these were man's first choice.

It is interesting to me that the ones whom God used the most in the Scriptures were those who were not the first choice of man. David was the youngest of his brethren. Saul came from the smallest tribe of Israel. Paul considered himself the least of the apostles. Peter was the one who made the greatest failures. Study the Scriptures and you will find these people didn't have to be humbled because they had no reason to be proud. Their humility caught God's attention which helped them overcome average.

One of the things that keeps those humble who overcome average is that they are not usually the ones voted as the most likely to succeed. Instead, they are the ones whose success surprised everyone. They overcame the obstacles they faced in life and truly overcame average.

Let me be an encouragement to you if others are always chosen to be used before you. This is not a bad thing, but it is God's way of keeping you humble.

I would rather be the least expected to succeed than to be the one who is expected to succeed and fail. God says in Proverbs 25:7, *"For better it is that it be said unto thee, Come up hither; than that thou shouldest be put lower in the presence of the prince whom thine eyes have seen."*

2. Each of these never forgot their humble beginnings.

David never forgot that he was a shepherd boy who watched his father's flock. Throughout Gideon's life he always remembered he was not the most likely to succeed. Moses always remembered that God called him out of the wilderness, and many times was willing to give his leadership over to others because he never forgot his humble beginnings.

One of the things that helps someone overcome average is never forgetting from whence they came. You will often hear successful business people tell people about their humble beginnings. Many great men of God consistently talk about their humble beginnings. Never forget from whence you came. If you will always remember your beginnings, you will not struggle with staying humble.

3. Each of these thought others were more qualified.

Isn't it interesting that Saul didn't want to be king? He wasn't the one lining up to be the first king;

rather, he was hiding in the bushes so the prophet would choose someone else. Moses kept trying to get God to use someone else, but He wanted Moses because he was humble enough to realize that he didn't deserve that position.

When a person has an attitude that others are more qualified, this will keep them humble enough to realize they need God. As long as you never forget that you truly need God, then you will be able to keep a humble spirit so God can use you. It's not that you are ignorant, but it is the fact that you know there are always others who can take your place. When you lose that attitude, God has a way of reminding you that there are others who are better than you.

4. Each of these were not afraid to submit themselves to their authorities.

This is such an important part of overcoming average. Nobody overcomes average on their own. They will always overcome average with the help of many others. This is why it is important to be humble enough to submit yourself to the authorities God places over your life.

When you look at your life, you will find there are many people whom God has placed along the path of your life to help you overcome average. There are your parents, pastor, Sunday school teacher, school teachers and others whom God placed in your life to help you overcome average. If you are not humble enough to submit yourself to them, then you will miss out on the contributions they can make to your life in helping you overcome average.

Stop questioning the authorities in your life, and submit to them so you can benefit from the contributions they have to offer you. Each authority was placed in your life to contribute something to help you overcome average. It is your responsibility to submit to them and find out what that contribution is. You will never overcome average if you are not humble enough to submit yourself to the authorities God has placed over you.

5. Each of these were willing to take advice from others.

This truly shows the humility of those who overcame average. David took advice from Samuel, Nathan and Joab. Saul took advice from Samuel. Moses took advice from his father-in-law. Paul took advice from the other apostles. Each of these could have looked at their position and thought they knew more than others; instead, they were humble enough to take advice from others who were their subordinates.

Being humble enough to take advice from others is critical to overcoming average. If you're too proud to take advice from followers or subordinates, then you will find yourself becoming average. Everyone can see something that you cannot see, and being humble enough to take their advice will only be beneficial to overcoming average.

6. Each of these pointed to God more than themselves.

Each of the men in the Scriptures whom God used mightily understood, *"He must increase, but I must decrease."* (John 3:30) They each understood they were God's representatives, and they were humble enough to always point their followers to God.

The degree of your humility can often be seen by how much you build up God in the minds of your followers. If you talk more about yourself, what you have and what you have done than you do about Who God is, what He has for others and what He has done for you, then you truly have your priorities mixed up. The more you lift up Christ to this world, the more God will help you overcome average.

On the other hand, the greatest enemy of humility is haughtiness and pride. Proverbs 16:18 says, *"Pride goeth before destruction, and an haughty spirit before a fall."* Haughtiness is having an arrogant attitude, and pride is thinking you're bigger than man and God. Pride and haughtiness is the quickest way to lose God's blessings on your life. When Saul became haughty and filled with pride, he saw his influence destroyed and eventually fell. A man who had so much potential saw it destroyed because of his haughtiness and pride.

THE HUMILITY OF OVERACHIEVERS

You are never bigger than God. If you want to overcome average, then you are going to have to keep a proper perspective of yourself. Yes, the more you accomplish for God the more confidence you will have in what you do, but don't let your confidence destroy your humility. Humility is one of the greatest contributing factors to overcoming average.

18

It's All About Attitude

Half of the battle that we fight in the Christian life is with our attitude. Your attitude determines how high you will rise in life. You attitude is a choice. Nobody makes you have a good attitude and nobody makes you have a bad attitude. Your attitude is completely reliant upon what you choose to do.

An airplane has many instruments that the pilot is to follow. One of the important instruments to follow is the attitude indicator. This instrument tells the pilot which way the nose of the airplane is pointed. It is interesting that they call it the attitude indicator. This instrument is very important when you are flying in the clouds because you have no horizon to judge which way you are going other than that instrument. You are always safer having the attitude pointing towards the sky when you are in the clouds because you never know what is underneath those clouds.

Those who overcome average tend to have an attitude indicator that points upward. You will find those who overcome average tend to have a great outlook on life. They are not normally people who are negative about life, but they are people who have a great attitude and outlook about everything they face in life. They don't complain, instead they always find a way to have a good attitude.

Philippians 4:13 says, *"I can do all things through Christ which strengtheneth me."* The first two words in this verse are important to the rest of the verse. The words, *"I can"* are an attitude. You will never be able to do all things without having an "I can" attitude. Your accomplishments in life are truly dependent upon your attitude of whether you believe you can.

When I was a boy, one of the words we could not use in our household was "can't." Truthfully, I hate hearing people say that it can't be done. They have already accepted failure as soon as they say, "Can't." My mother used to tell me to find a way to do something instead of saying, "I can't do it."

Christopher Columbus would have never discovered America if he had an "I can't" attitude. There were many in his day who believed discovering a new world could not happen, but he kept the "I can" attitude in spite of the negativity that surrounded him. The "I can" attitude helped him in discovering America.

The American forefathers had an "I can" attitude about pulling away from England. What many don't understand about the American revolution is that those who believed America should pull away from England were the minority. About a third of the country was loyal to the king and didn't want to pull away. Another third of the country either didn't care or didn't want to get involved. It was the last third of the country who believed it could happen, and that attitude helped them to forge a way to victory.

Thomas Edison had an "I can" attitude about developing a light bulb. They said he failed to develop at fluorescent light bulb over a thousand times, but he never lost the "I can" attitude that drove him to find a way. Because of his "I can" attitude, a whole world enjoys lights in their homes.

The apostles certainly had an "I can" attitude about reaching the world for Christ. It seemingly looked as though they would never reach the world because of the angst against Jesus Christ, but they forged on with their "I can" attitude. They overcame beatings, imprisonments and persecution with an "I can" attitude which led them to turn the world upside down for Christ.

It all comes down to your attitude. If you are going to overcome average, then you must have the "I can" attitude of Philippians 4:13. Without the "I can" attitude, you will slip off into the average. The average come up with excuses. The average say it can't be done. The average quit when faced with overwhelming obstacles. The average look at the giants of life and say they are too big to conquer. They see the hardships and easily give in because they don't have the attitude that they can do it.

Those who overcome average will always have an "I can" attitude. There are several steps you must take to help you develop the "I can" attitude.

1. You must take personal responsibility for your own actions.

The first word in Philippians 4:13 is, "I". You must take personal responsibility for your own actions if you are going to develop the "I can" attitude. Personal responsibility drives you to have a right attitude. It tells you to stop blaming everyone else for your problems and situation in life and determine to do something about it yourself.

The "I can" attitude puts the responsibility for changing your situation solely upon your shoulders. The "I can" attitude causes you to stop looking for someone else to pull you out of your situation. Nobody else is going to care as much about what you do in life than you. Stop looking for someone to bail you out and simply develop the "I can" attitude.

2. Stop comparing yourself to others.

One of the reasons people struggle with an "I can" attitude is because they have lived their lives comparing themselves to others. They think they can't do something because they are not as smart as someone else. They feel they are not as talented as someone else. They look at their resources and believe they could never do something because they don't have as much as someone else has. They have a defeatist attitude because they are too busy comparing themselves to others.

God says, *"For we dare not make ourselves of the number, or compare ourselves with some that commend themselves: but they measuring themselves by themselves, and comparing themselves among themselves, are not wise."* (2 Corinthians 10:12) Stop looking at what others have and start realizing that God gave you the resources you need to accomplish what He has called you to do. When you realize that God made you the way you are to do what He created you to do, then you will find it easier to have an "I can" attitude. Always remember that someone looks at you and wishes they had what you have. Don't let your perception of your shortcomings defeat your attitude. You will only develop the "I can" attitude by accepting yourself the way God made you.

3. Don't listen to the negative voices.

There are going to be many negative voices in your life that will try to defeat your attitude. Nehemiah had to overcome the negative voices of Tobiah and Sanballat. David had to overcome the negative voice of his brother Eliab. Saul had to overcome the negative voices of men who didn't believe he could be king. Noah had to overcome the negative voices of a society that said there would be no rain.

You cannot develop an "I can" attitude when you allow yourself to listen to the negative voices in your life. The negative voices will always seem to be louder than the voices that encourage you. Developing an "I can" attitude can only be accomplished by turning a deaf ear towards the negative voices in your life.

4. Take action on your faith.

Action has a way of giving you a good attitude. Philippians 4:13 says, *"I can **do** all things through Christ..."* The third word in this verse is an action word. Action always brings a better attitude than inaction. Action gives excitement. Action gives hope. Action says you believe it can happen. Action is the belief that your faith is real.

As long as you sit and wait for everything to fall into place before you do what God wants you to do, you will always have a negative attitude. Taking action on your faith gives the "I can" attitude. Many times the only solid thing you can bank on when you step out by faith other than God is your "I can" attitude. Make action a key part of your life and you will find you will have the right attitude.

5. Build off smaller accomplishments.

One of the things you will have to do to develop an "I can" attitude is to look at what you have already accomplished, and use that as your springboard to stretch yourself to do greater things for God. David did this when he faced Goliath. He looked at the smaller accomplishments of defeating the lion and bear, and that gave him the courage to believe he could defeat Goliath. One may wonder if he would have ever fought Goliath had he not built his "I can" attitude from his smaller accomplishments.

There is always a smaller accomplishment in your life from which you can build the confidence that God can do something through you. All it takes is faith the size of a mustard seed to give you the faith to move mountains in your life. Don't discount the smaller accomplishments, but use them to help you develop the "I can" attitude. They will encourage you to move the mountains in your life if you will let them.

6. Only be satisfied with your best.

The only pressure you need to put upon yourself is the pressure to do your best. God does not require success, but He requires you to do your best. He says in Colossians 3:23, *"And whatsoever ye do, do it heartily, as to the Lord, and not unto men;"* Many people discourage themselves because they are success driven instead of simply doing their best. Nobody can guarantee success, but you can guarantee that you can do your best. When you use the standard of doing your best at whatever you do, then you will find yourself overcoming a negative attitude. You know you can do your best, and as long as you do that, then you can have the right attitude.

7. Ask yourself the right question.

One of the biggest reasons we have the wrong attitude is because we ask ourselves the wrong questions. Instead of asking yourself why it can't be done, you need to ask what you can do to make it happen. Look beyond the "can't" and ask yourself how it "can" be done.

Matthew 17:20 says, *"And Jesus said unto them, Because of your unbelief: for verily I say unto you, If ye have faith as a grain of mustard seed, ye shall say unto this mountain, Remove hence to yonder place; and it shall remove; and nothing shall be impossible unto you."* God is teaching the importance in this verse of finding a way to make it happen. He says their unbelief caused the mountain not to be moved.

When you start asking yourself how it can be done, then your attitude will become an "I can" attitude. "I can" attitudes look at how it can happen and not at why it can't happen. Don't let the voices of doubt and fear keep you from having the attitude that it can be done.

8. Equip yourself with knowledge.

Why do people have such negative attitudes that say it can never happen? Usually it is because they don't have the knowledge of how to do what needs to get done. Romans 15:4 says, *"For whatsoever things were written aforetime were written for our learning, that we through patience and comfort of the scriptures might have hope."* Knowledge gives confidence, and confidence brings an "I can" attitude.

Stop using your lack of knowledge as an excuse as to why it can't be done. If you lack the knowledge, then go and acquire the knowledge it takes to believe you can do it. A lack of knowledge is no one else's fault but your own. You can acquire the necessary knowledge if you will put your mind to it. When you have the knowledge of how something can be done, you will find it easier to have an "I can" attitude.

9. Don't accept failure.

Failure cannot be an option. Luke 1:37 says, *"For with God nothing shall be impossible."* Notice the word *"nothing."* That means God expects His children not to accept failure because He can truly help you succeed. With God all things are possible; therefore, failure cannot be an option. You must have the attitude that you are going to make it or die trying to. Failure is the attitude of the average and victory is the only option of those who have an "I can" attitude.

10. Get God on your side.

You will never keep the right attitude without getting God on your side. Look at Philippians 4:13

again, *"I can do all things through Christ which strengtheneth me."* Notice that the "I can" is totally dependent upon doing everything through the power of Christ. You can't do everything in your own power, but you can do everything through the power of Jesus Christ.

When you get God's power working through you, it is like lighting a stick of dynamite that blows up every obstacle in your pathway. We get our word "dynamite" from the words, *"which strengtheneth me."* God says, when you develop the "I can" attitude and do something about it with His help, it is like lighting a stick of dynamite to every obstacle you face in life.

How do you develop an "I can" attitude to remove the mountains in your life? Simply believe it can be done, take action and do it with God's help. The ten steps in this chapter are key to developing an "I can" attitude. Overcoming average is all about attitude; it is all about having the "I can" attitude.

19

IT'S NOT ABOUT YOU

Several years ago, I was taking a trip from Seattle to Chicago. My flight was supposed to be later in the afternoon. When I arrived at the airport, the dreaded notification on my flight said, "DELAYED." This is normally not that bad of news until they continually delay the flight. After a couple of hours of delays, the agent at the desk made the much dreaded announcement: "This flight has been cancelled."

Frustrated, I made my way to the Red Carpet Club to see if I could get on a flight the next morning. They worked with me and gave me a seat in first class on a flight that left out early in the morning, and they also gave me a voucher for a hotel that night. After calling my wife and giving her the news, I went to the hotel to get a good nights rest.

The next morning I woke up early and went to the airport to board my flight back to Chicago. I got situated in my seat and was wondering who would be the person sitting next to me. In walked a young man who had piercings all over his body and headphones in his ears. His hat somehow must have been bumped because it wasn't on his head correctly. He looked up at the row in which I was sitting, and my honest thoughts were, "Please LORD, let me have someone else sit next to me." Well, the LORD didn't answer my prayer. This young man proceeded to settle in his seat, and before I could even greet him, he had closed his eyes to go to sleep for the long flight.

The trip went relatively well, and the person next to me didn't bother me one bit. We started our descent, and the young man finally woke up. I greeted him and began to talk to him. After a few minutes of conversation, I asked him if he knew he would go to Heaven if he were to die. He responded that he did not know where he would go, but wanted to know. In the next few minutes, I showed this young man how to be saved.

After I gave him assurance of his salvation, he asked me if I would do something for him. Tears were running down this young man's face as he told me that he just left his father in Seattle to go back to live with his mother in the Chicago area. He asked me to have someone go by his father's house and tell him the same thing that he learned on that flight. He told me his father was struggling and needed the same assurance that he just received.

Immediately, the conviction hit my heart about complaining about my flight the night before. I realized that it was not all about me. God cancelled my flight because He knew that young man would be on that flight and needed to get saved. God knew that young man would be concerned with his father's eternal destiny, so He cancelled my flight so that young man could hear the greatest news that he would ever hear; the Gospel of Jesus Christ.

Friend, life is truly not about you. We live in a world where it seems many people are wrapped up in their own little world. People walk down the street or the airport terminals not paying attention to anyone else but themselves. Drivers drive down the street in their own little world not considering that there are other people on the roads. If you're not careful, you will get hit or run over by people driving or walking in their own little world.

This world has become so self-centered that people truly believe life revolves around them. They walk around never looking up, and could care less if they are walking in someone's path. They drive carelessly in their own little world never thinking about changing lanes when others are coming onto the highway. I know these are just a couple of illustrations, but people have become so self-centered that they never look up to notice there are others in the world beside them.

John 4:35 says, *"Say not ye, There are yet four months, and then cometh harvest? behold, I say unto you, Lift up your eyes, and look on the fields; for they are white already to harvest."* Notice God's command to *"lift up your eyes."* God knew that people would become self-centered. He knew they would make life all about them, and that self-centered attitude would keep them from seeing the greatest need in the world; the need of a Saviour. He commanded the Christian to lift up their eyes so they could realize that life is not all about them.

Those who overcome average quickly understand that life is not all about them. You will live an average life if you make everything about yourself. There are several observations you need to see about this topic if you are going to overcome average.

1. The world does not revolve around you.

Have you ever thought that you are one of seven billion people in the world? To live your life as if this world is all about you is truly absurd. God did not place you on the Earth for you. He placed you on this Earth to fulfill His plan. This world does not revolve around you, your wishes or desires. There are so many other people in this world other than you.

You will never overcome average when your life revolves around you. Those who overcome average do so by making their life about others. Look at the mindset of our Saviour, *"Let this mind be in you, which was also in Christ Jesus: Who, being in the form of God, thought it not robbery to be equal with God: But made himself of no reputation, and took upon him the form of a servant, and was made in the likeness of men:"* (Philippians 2:5-7) Jesus truly forgot about Himself and made the world His agenda. That act of selflessness is what changed the world forever. Without that selfless example, every person would be in trouble.

If the Saviour can live a selfless life, then we certainly should follow His example. Jesus told the disciples after they were squabbling about sitting beside Him in His kingdom, *"But so shall it not be among you: but whosoever will be great among you, shall be your minister: And whosoever of you will be the chiefest, shall be servant of all."* (Mark 10:43-44) The only way you can overcome average is to completely forget about yourself and serve others.

2. Think about others before you act.

The greatest contributor to people being average is that every act is based upon their own wants, wishes and desires. The average won't serve God because it doesn't agree with their schedule. The average won't be hospitable because it will inconvenience them. The average quit because what they are doing is too hard and takes too much time. Every action of the average is a result of how it affects them.

On the other hand, those who overcome average think about how their actions will affect those around them. They give up preferences because someone else may not prefer it. They yield to another's wishes when it comes to opinions. They think about the long term affects their decisions will have on others and whether it affects them adversely or favorably.

When Jesus prayed to the Father when He was facing the cross He said, "...O my Father, if it be possible, let this cup pass from me: nevertheless not as I will, but as thou wilt." (Matthew 26:39) Jesus knew quitting would affect others, so He did not quit for the world's sake.

Everything you do every day should be tempered by how it will affect others. Before you spend money on something frivolous, how will it affect your family? Drive your car with the mindset of how your driving affects others on the road. Walk through public places with an alertness about how every step you take affects others. Simply be cognizant of the fact that you are not the only one in the world. Realize there are others around you. Be perceptive with every move you make and how that move will affect others.

3. Lift up your eyes and see.

One of the key commands in the Scriptures is found in John 4:35 when the Saviour says, "...Lift up your eyes, and look on the fields; for they are white already to harvest." You will never see the needs of others until you lift up your eyes. One of the things that contributed to the disciples squabbling was that they had not lifted up their eyes to see the need of the world. When they lifted their eyes, they saw the need all about them, and they laid aside their self-centered lifestyles to try and fulfill the needs of the world.

If you will lift up your eyes, you will see there are people all around you who have needs that only you can meet. Those who overcome average have lifted their eyes, saw the needs of others and met them. That need may have been a physical need, or it could have been their need of a Saviour. You will never overcome average while looking down at yourself. You will only overcome average by lifting your eyes up and seeing the needs of this world.

Furthermore, you need to lift up your ears and hear what people are saying to you. Don't be so wrapped up in your little world that you don't hear when people are talking to you. Listen to people as they talk. Those who overcome average hear what others do not hear because they are listening. They hear and act upon the needs they hear; thus, they met the need when the average didn't even notice that their was a need. If you will listen, you will hear the needs of others. Pay attention when people talk to you.

4. Deflect credit when it comes your way.

One of the great attributes about those who overcome average is that they normally deflect credit given away from themselves. When credit is given, they deflect the attention to those who've helped them to succeed.

King David spent a whole chapter talking about his mighty men. He could have talked about all that he had done, but instead he deflected the credit to those who would have never been recognized otherwise. Many of the psalms are an act of deflecting credit from man to God. One of the characteristics that truly helped David overcome average was his willingness to deflect the credit given him on others.

The next time someone gives you credit, find someone else who helped you and deflect it towards them. When people see that you are not afraid to share the credit with others, then they will be more likely to help you achieve great projects. You cannot do everything by yourself. You need the help of others. So, when credit comes your way after a success, learn to deflect that credit to others.

5. It doesn't always have to be your way.

Those who overcome average truly understand their way is not the only way. I'm not talking about truth, but I am talking about preference. The average always has to have things done their way. It doesn't matter that someone else may have a better idea, the average foolishly forces their own way to their own detriment.

Those who overcome average are pleased when others get their way. We have already pointed out that Jesus wanted the Father to have His way when it came to the cross. God says in Ephesians 5:21, *"Submitting yourselves one to another in the fear of God."* (Ephesians 5:21) God is simply commanding us to let others have their way. You will find this verse is talking about relationships. Submit yourself and let others have their way. This is a characteristic of those who overcome average.

If you want your ministry to thrive, then you must not make it about you or your legacy. Those whom God has used greatly in the ministry realized that the ministry was all about serving others. They did not use their ministry to serve themselves, but they used their ministry to serve others. This is what turns an average ministry into a great ministry. When each pastor or ministry leader stops pointing to themselves and uses their ministry to meet the needs of those whom they serve, then they will find their ministry will become greater than they ever imagined.

The person who doesn't make their relationships with others all about themselves will find fulfillment in each relationship. The greatest kind of relationships are those that are not about what you can get out of it, but what you can do to meet the other persons needs. The greatest relationships are those in which a person truly tries to meet the needs of another.

The best business model is the model that tries to meet the needs of the customer. When the needs of the customer are met, it is amazing how the customer will keep coming back. The greatest businesses are the ones that found out the needs of their customers and met or exceeded those needs. This business model works every time.

Friend, if you want to overcome average, then you must not make life about you. You must lift up your eyes and see that God is using you as a tool to meet the needs of others. If you keep your eyes on yourself, you will gripe and complain about how bad life is. If you will realize that life is not about you, then you'll see that God places you in the right place at your inopportune time to meet the need of someone else. Don't miss those opportunities because you are living in your own little world. Come out of your little world and see the needs of others. This will help propel you towards overcoming average.

20

YOU NEED A BOSS

There are two people who have different outcomes to their day. The first person never has enough time to get things done. Though their responsibilities are not that great, they always seem to run out of time and never accomplish what they are supposed to do. The other person is highly productive. They seem to have more on their plate than anyone else, but they always fulfill their responsibilities. They handle more than the first person. They have more responsibilities than the first person. They always seem to have enough time to do everything. They are definitely busier than the first person.

So, what is the difference between the two? The difference is the first person has no schedule and only accomplishes what has to be done at the last minute. The second person has a schedule and lets their schedule organize their life so they don't have wasted time. The lack of schedule causes the first person to live a stressed-out unproductive life, while the second person's stress level is very low and seems to truly enjoy life. The whole difference is that one chooses to schedule their day and let their schedule be their boss, while the first person is disorganized and only takes care of what they can at the last minute. One has a schedule that helps them accomplish more than the one who has less responsibilities.

Those who overcome average have learned the value of time management. One of the greatest contributing factors to their accomplishments is that they live by schedule. They get the most out of every day because their schedule helps them to accomplish more. There are people more talented and educated than they, but the one who overcomes average is able to accomplish more than anyone else because they have a schedule.

Everybody has seven days in a week, one hundred and sixty-eight hours in each week, twenty-four hours in a day and sixty minutes in each hour. Nobody has more time than another. Yet, when you look at what is accomplished in these time frames by those who overcome average, you will find that very little of their time is wasted. They have learned the value of scheduling their life and letting that schedule be their boss.

Everybody must have a boss over their time. Many adults never learned from their school days that schedule was important to their degree. They had a time they started and finished. They had a time for breaks and study. Their day was planned for them, and that is why they were able to get their studies done. Sadly, when most adults graduate, they forsake the schedule that was important for thirteen years during their undergraduate studies. If they were to apply that schedule back into their life, they would find they would get back to completing all their daily tasks and projects.

Schedule is so important to life that God implemented one on the very first day of creation. Genesis 1:5 says, *"And God called the light Day, and the darkness he called Night. And the evening and the morning were the first day."* Every day you live there is a morning and night. That is scheduled into your life by God. Every year there are seasons. This is all God's scheduling. Every day the sun rises in the morning and sets at night. This is schedule. God set this world on a schedule for the sake of the Earth producing crops and vegetation. God knows that everything needs a schedule.

Ephesians 5:16 says, *"Redeeming the time, because the days are evil."* Time is a valuable commodity that must not be wasted. Every minute that passes by cannot be retrieved. That is why God commands us to redeem the time. The word *"redeeming"* means, to rescue from loss. In other words, God wants to keep every Christian from losing one second of their life. The only way you will do this is to live by a schedule.

Scheduling is an art that many never master. Those who master the art of scheduling will find themselves able to accomplish more in their lifetime. The more you are able to accomplish in life, the better chance you have of overcoming average. There are several keys to learn in mastering the art of scheduling.

1. Ask God's guidance in creating a schedule.

God is the giver of time. Because He is the giver of time, He knows best how you should use your time. Ecclesiastes chapter 3 shows us that there is a time for everything to be done.

God says, *"If any of you lack wisdom, let him ask of God, that giveth to all men liberally, and upbraideth not; and it shall be given him."* (James 1:5) You certainly don't know what each day holds; therefore, you need God's wisdom to help you plan your day. Before you ever begin to work on your schedule, ask for God's guidance and wisdom as you approach your day.

2. Determine what you must get done.

Ecclesiastes 3:1 says, *"To every thing there is a season, and a time to every purpose under the heaven:"* Everything must be categorized in your life as to when it needs to be done. You will find that everything will fall into the categorical times of, daily, weekly, monthly and yearly.

Everything you must do will fall under one of these categories. I know you may not be able to remember everything that needs to be done, but you would be wise to take an overview of your life and write down everything you need to do and what category of time it falls under. If you will get your time categorized, it will help you streamline your scheduling more efficiently.

3. Determine the priorities of what must be done.

Everything you do has a level of importance. The Scriptures help us in learning the level of importance. For instance, we know from Matthew 6:33 that God is to be the first priority in our lives. Before you do anything in the day, you must spend time with God.

After God comes family. After the world was created, God made man in His image. God instituted the first home in the Book of Genesis. So, family must carry a high level of importance in your priorities. After the family comes the church. Again, when you get these priorities right, you will find your scheduling becomes easier.

Life has it priorities, and you must determine those priorities before you begin your scheduling. Always remember that work comes before pleasure. (2 Thessalonians 3:10) Every task and project you must perform each day has a level of importance. Write them down in the order of their importance.

4. Create an action plan for each task.

If you are going to use your time efficiently, then you must create a sequence of events for each scheduled task. If you don't have a sequence of events written down, you will find yourself wasting valuable time trying to figure out how to approach a project or meeting.

For instance, if you have a meeting with someone, write down in order what you are going to discuss in that meeting. This will help the meeting to be run more efficiently, and will keep it organized so you don't waste time trying to figure out what you are going to do next.

5. Let your schedule be your boss.

You must submit to your schedule. There is no purpose in having a schedule if you are not going to obey it. When your schedule dictates that you must do something, then you have to obey it. If something is not in your schedule, then you must not let it steal your time.

There are many time wasters in life. If you don't guard your time with your schedule, then the time wasters will steal precious minutes from you. Always remember that all it takes to lose an hour in your day is to lose one minute sixty times. If you want to get the most out of your time, then you must submit yourself to your schedule.

6. Schedule routines.

The first thing you start scheduling are your routines. There are daily routines and there are weekly routines. These are things you will do everyday and every week.

Your daily routines should consist of scheduling a time to get up every day. I believe it's wise to get up at the same time every day. Part of your daily routines also consist of your walk with God, meals, bed time and a time to relax.

Your weekly routines will include every church service, time with your family and a time with your spouse. Of course, there are going to be things on the job you must do weekly, and these would be included in the weekly routines. Routine tasks must be scheduled or they will either be forgotten or considered unimportant.

7. Write your schedule down.

A schedule kept in your mind is not a schedule. You must write down what you are going to do. In today's world of technology, writing your schedule down is much easier. Whether you write it on a daily planner that you keep on your desk or write it down electronically, it is important that it is something you can look at so you will know what you are to do at each time of the day.

8. Work on the present project.

It will be easy to become sidetracked with other projects you have throughout the day if you don't develop a mindset to give your full attention to the present task. Don't worry about the next project until it is time to work on it. Give your full attention and energies to what is on your schedule for the present. You will never accomplish each task efficiently if you are wandering back and forth between projects. One of the reasons you have a schedule is so that you can give your full attention to the task at hand so it can be accomplished in a timely fashion.

9. Create deadlines.

Deadlines are the key to scheduling. If you don't have a deadline for something to be done, then you will never accomplish it. Deadlines motivate you to stay focused. Deadlines dictate the level of importance. Deadlines keep procrastination and laziness in check. You might be prone to procrastination and laziness, but deadlines will help you to overcome those weaknesses.

One of the reasons you have a payment schedule for your mortgage is because the bank knows you would never pay your bill if you didn't have a deadline. If deadlines work for paying bills, then deadlines will work for your daily schedule. Everything you do must have a deadline associated with it or it will never be completed.

10. Schedule times wisely.

There are certain times of the day and week that are better to handle projects and tasks. You must study yourself to know when is the best time to accomplish certain responsibilities and tasks. You are unique, and learning how to handle certain situations and projects when you are at your best is an important component of completing things in a timely fashion.

You need to learn when you are the most alert. Normally, this will be the first part of every day. That is a great time for you to handle the harder tasks. Right after lunch is not a good time to handle assignments that take full mental focus because you will normally be a bit sluggish. Learn to handle the harder projects that demand attention when you are most alert.

Furthermore, deal with situations that require more time to heal emotionally at the right time. There are certain times every week when you must be at your best. Don't schedule meetings that will negatively affect your emotions right before those meetings. Learn your emotional recovery time, and schedule the projects and meetings that negatively affect your emotions well in advance of the time you need to be emotionally strong.

11. Schedule unpleasant tasks sooner rather than later.

One of the keys to scheduling and making your day more pleasant and productive is to get the unpleasant tasks accomplished at the beginning of the day. When completing the unpleasant tasks early in your day, the rest of the day will be more pleasant. On the other hand, when you put off the unpleasant tasks until the end of the day, you create an unpleasant outlook towards your day. Get the unpleasantries done earlier, and the rest of the schedule will be easier.

12. Don't waste transition time.

One of the areas where many people waste time is during transition. Driving in your car is a transition time. Instead of wasting that time, schedule phone appointments and return calls during that time. This is a great way to use your time to its fullest.

One of the keys in determining whether or not you will overcome average is your use of time. If you will learn to use a schedule and let your schedule be your boss, you will find yourself accomplishing more which will enable you to do more than the average. Don't let your time be stolen from you because of a lack of schedule; instead, redeem your time to its fullest by using a daily schedule.

21

GET BACK UP

The fear that most people face when asked to do something or when needed to do something is failure. Nobody wants to be a failure. You never find a person who wakes up in the morning and has the desire to fail that day. We all want to succeed. The problem is that we are going to fail. As hard as you try to avoid failure, it is going to come. The determining factor of whether or not you overcome average is what you do when you have failed. If you lie in your failure then you will become average. If you decide to get back up, you will be one of the few who overcome average.

Failure is a misused word. The world often defines a failure as one who was unsuccessful in an endeavor. On the other had, God defines a failure as one who simply refuses to get back up. In other words, a failure is one who quits. Just because you didn't succeed in a venture does not make you a failure as long as you choose to get back up.

Proverbs 24:16 says, *"For a just man falleth seven times, and riseth up again: but the wicked shall fall into mischief."* The key to the just man in this verse is that he kept getting back up. He was not a failure.

The thing that kept him from becoming a failure is the fact that he got up one more time than he fell. He may have failed in his finances, but he got back up and tried to become financially stable again. He may have failed in overcoming temptation, but he got back up and determined to do his best not to yield to temptation the next time. He may have failed in his ministry, but he got back up and was resolved to do better in that ministry. He may have failed in a relationship, but he was determined to get back up and do his part not to hurt the relationship again.

The just man fell, and he got back up. He fell again, but he got back up. He fell again, but he didn't sulk in his failure and got back up. The one action this just man knew how to do very well was to get back up. He understood that if he got up one more time than he fell then he would eventually succeed.

Friend, the key to overcoming average is getting back up. Every person who has overcome average has fallen at one point in their life. The difference between them and others is they got back up when others quit. Let me give you several thoughts on failure and getting back up.

1. Failure only comes to those who attempt to do something.

It's easy to criticize those who've failed, but the only reason they failed is because they attempted to do something. A person who never attempts anything never fails. You can only miss hitting the target if you tried hitting it to begin with. So, you didn't hit the bullseye, but at least you tried. The only reason you experienced failure is because you tried to do something while the critic sat on the sideline watching your attempt. Monday morning quarterbacking is easy when you were not on the field facing the pressures of the battle.

So, you failed in business. At least you attempted a business adventure when others did not. So, you failed in a ministry. At least you tried to do something for God when others sat on the sideline watching. So, you failed to walk with God regularly. At least you attempted to have a regular walk with God when others have never even tried. Stop feeling bad about your failure, for at least you tried when others did not.

2. Most success is preceded by failure.

One of the best kept secrets about success is that most people fail before they ever succeed. They said that Thomas Edison failed many times to invent a light bulb, but he kept getting back up and made another attempt at this invention. We enjoy his success every day, but we often fail to remember that his success was preceded by failure.

Michael Jordan is arguably considered the greatest basketball player to ever play professional basketball. What many don't realize about him is that he was cut from his high school basketball team. Instead of allowing that failure to keep him down, he got back up and developed a practice ethic that propelled him into the NBA, and which eventually brought him six national championships and a name among the greatest in his sport. Yes, we've enjoyed his success, but it was preceded by failure.

There is nothing wrong with being a failure, but there is something wrong with being a quitter. We put way too much emphasis on failure. I would rather have someone on my team who has failed a thousand times than a person who has quit one time. If you will realize that success is built through failure, then you can get back up with dignity and try again.

3. Strength is built through failure.

One of the hobbies I have enjoyed throughout my life is lifting weights. Anyone who has lifted weights will understand the term, "Lifting to failure." In other words, you keep lifting the weight until you fail to lift it because you have no more strength. What many don't realize is that the failure to lift that weight the last time will build the strength needed to lift it the next time.

You can either let failure destroy you, or you can learn from your failure and not make the same mistake again. Study what caused your failure and don't do the same thing again. Every time you fail, you are learning what to avoid the next time.

So, you failed. If you will get up one more time than you fail, you will eventually discover success. You will never find success without failure. Failure is a part of success, so don't let it destroy you.

4. Failure simply means you are one step closer to success.

Most of us have taken tests that had multiple choice questions. The great thing about this type of test is that you can only fail it three times before you discover the formula of success by default. You may have failed the test once, but you are one step closer to success because you've found one answer that is not right. You can choose the next two answers that are wrong, but every time you get back up you are one step closer to success.

If you keep getting back up and doing something different than before, then you are getting closer to finding what helps you overcome average. Don't let the multiple failures keep you from getting up and attempting something else. Always remember that failure is a reminder that you are one step closer to success. You have learned one more thing that causes failure, which means you have eliminated one more way to fail.

5. Failure only makes a person a failure if they quit.

True failure is quitting. If you don't want to be a failure, then don't quit. It is the quitter who has become the failure. You may have failed a hundred times, but as long as you keep getting back up you have not become a failure by God's definition.

The only way you can fail at winning someone to Christ is to quit trying to lead people to Christ. The only way you can fail at overcoming a besetting sin is to quit trying to overcome it. The only way you can fail at being a good spouse is if you quit trying to be a good spouse. The only way you can fail at being a good parent is if you stop trying to be a good parent. Truly, the only way you can fail is if you quit.

6. Don't allow the fear of failure to hold you back from attempting something.

There are two things that keep a person from attempting something, and one of those is the fear of failure. Many people will never attempt anything because they are afraid they are going to fail. Let me be honest with you. You are going to fail! You might as well get over it. If you step out and attempt to do anything, you are going to fail, but don't let the fear of failure hold you back.

One of the biggest reasons people won't serve God is because they are afraid they will fail. They won't teach a Sunday school class because they are afraid of failure. A young man won't attempt to start a church because he is afraid he may fail. A Christian won't go soul winning because they are afraid of someone rejecting their attempt to lead them to

Christ. Those who overcome average will not listen to the voice of fear, but they step out by faith understanding they will experience failure. When failure comes, they get back up and attempt it again.

7. Don't let failure keep you from attempting great things again.

I said there were two things that keep people from attempting things, and the second one is failing. This person didn't listen to the voice of fear and they stepped out and attempted something, but they failed. When they failed, they did not like the bitter taste of failure, so they vowed they would never attempt something like that again.

Friend, you must not let the bitter taste of failure hold you back from attempting great things for God. The bitter taste of failure makes the taste of success that much sweeter if you will get back up. Failure may be embarrassing and humbling, but swallow your pride and get up.

Nearly every week of my life I travel somewhere and preach revival meetings or conferences. Oftentimes, I hear the praise of sincere people who have found my sermon was helpful. What they don't realize is the great failure I experienced the first time I preached. I was given a thirty minute time slot to fill. I had studied and filled out several pages of notes. I wondered as I studied how I would ever finish the whole sermon in thirty minutes. When I got up to preach, my sermon lasted five minutes before I was through with all of my notes. Now, I had twenty-five minutes left to fill with nothing to say. Needless to say, it was a colossal failure, but I got up and preached again. Now, God uses me to help people around the country, and that only happens because I didn't let my failure hold me down.

Don't let your failure keep you down. You are going to fail, and the taste of failure is truly bitter; however, if you will get back up, you will eventually find God can use you mightily. The Scriptures are filled with people who got back up after failure. These people are no different than you and I. They served the same God you do, so get back up and keep on going in spite of failure.

8. When all else fails, get back up.

The whole key to overcoming average is getting up one more time. What I love about Proverbs 24:16 is that God says the just man falls *"seven times."* These two words are referring to a seven day week. Then it says he *"riseth up again."* In other words, he failed seven straight days, but got back up on Sunday and said, "I am going to start all over and try again."

When all else fails, the one thing you must do is get back up. You may not know how to do anything else real well, but you can certainly learn to get back up. Getting back up may be the thing you know the best, but at least you have not quit. When failure has knocked you down, and life's referee is giving the eight count, pull yourself back up if you must, but don't quit. Just get back up and keep taking one more step.

One last thing that is interesting about Proverbs 24:16 are the words, *"just man."* These words infer that they are going to balance the books. When you justify the books, you balance the books. In other words, those who overcome average get back up and determine to even the score. The Devil may have knocked you down, but you must determine you are going to get back up and even the score.

If you are going to overcome average, then there must be a fire inside of you to get back up when you experience failure. Don't let the fear of failure or the bitter taste of failure hold you down. Get back up and even the score. The one thing that will help you overcome average is not your talent, intellect or prowess, it is your ability and fortitude to get back up. If you want to overcome average, then you must be determined to always get back up when you have been knocked down.

22

WHAT'S THE SECRET?

Is there a secret to overcoming average? Is there some secret potion a person needs to purchase to overcome average? Is overcoming average only for a select few? This is what most would think. Most think that those who've overcome average were lucky, special or talented, but this is simply not true.

The secret to overcoming average is old-fashioned hard work. The "luckiest" people in the world are those who work hard. There is no secret to overcoming average. Overcoming average is not just for those who grow up with a silver spoon in their mouth. Anyone can overcome average.

If you grew up on the poor side of town, you can overcome average if you will put your mind to it and work hard. If you are not the most talented person, you can overcome average if you will develop a good work ethic. Hard work seems to overcome every shortcoming a person could have. It overcomes educational shortcomings, lack of talent, lack of resources, a poor background and lack of physical ability.

One of the most obvious characteristics that separates the average from those who overcome average is their work ethic. Those who overcome average often outwork the underachiever. Those who overcome average work longer and harder than the average. There is no secret to overcoming average. It is old fashioned hard work that propels them to success.

Some of the greatest overachievers in life seemed to be people who were blessed with talent when in reality they simply worked hard. Michael Jordan certainly seemed talented, but it was his offseason workouts that made him such a great basketball talent. During the offseason when others were busy spending their money, Michael Jordan spent his days taking hundreds of jump shots to improve his shooting ability.

Steve Jobs, one of the most recognized names in the technology world, never graduated from college. Even though some would say that lack of a college education will hinder you from success, Jobs figured out that he could outwork every person who had a college degree. It has been said that Mr. Jobs worked close to 90 hours a week in his prime. It is no wonder he became the great success.

Dr. Jack Hyles, a man whom God used to build the largest Sunday school in the world, was the first to say that he was not the most talented. He came from a poor background and was kicked out of the most recognized religious organization of his day, yet God used him to build the First Baptist Church in

Hammond, Indiana to over 15,000 attendees every Sunday in Sunday school. What was his secret? It was his work ethic. He said that he determined as a young man that though he was not as eloquent as other speakers, or as great of a leader as other pastors, that he could outwork them all. His work ethic is what helped him to overcome average.

These illustrations are not an endorsement of the lifestyles of the first two men, but it is simply showing that the secret to overcoming average is to develop a scriptural work ethic. You don't have to be talented if you will work hard. You don't have to have charisma as long as you work hard. Whatever your shortcoming may be, it can be overcome by developing a good work ethic. The Scriptures give us several observations about work that will help motivate you to develop a good work ethic.

1. Work is God-like.

One of the greatest ways a Christian can emulate God is by working. Genesis 2:2 says, *"And on the seventh day God ended his work which he had made..."* God is a worker. God worked six days and then rested on the seventh.

God created you in His image. That means if God was a worker, then He created you to be a worker. Genesis 2:15 says, *"And the Lord God took the man, and put him into the garden of Eden to dress it and to keep it."* You will never be satisfied with your life until you become a worker. If a Christian truly wants to be like God, then they should become a hard worker.

2. You'll never advance in life without working.

Advancement in life is a result of hard work. We live in days when people want to be promoted on the job because of seniority, but that is not scriptural. Proverbs 14:23 says, *"In all labour there is profit: but the talk of the lips tendeth only to penury."* A person should only be promoted because they've work hard.

Your work ethic will do more to advance you than any talent or ability. Talents and ability will eventually fall short, but a good work ethic will always be a part of a person's character. You will find that those who work harder are the ones who eventually end up with the best positions. They got those positions by earning them through hard work.

3. Working will make your meals taste better.

One of the great benefits of working hard is enjoying your meal after a day of hard work. Proverbs 12:11 says, *"He that tilleth his land shall be satisfied with bread..."* It is amazing how all meals taste good after a hard days work. Working creates an appetite, and the average meal becomes a great meal when you are hungry. Work harder if you want your meals to taste better.

4. Working cures sleep disorders.

One thing I've never understood is when people tell me they have a hard time going to sleep. My wife has said to me that she is amazed how quickly I go to sleep. The reason I go to sleep so quickly is because I start working early in the morning and go till late at night. I have always found it is not hard to sleep when you're tired from working hard. Ecclesiastes 5:12 says, *"The sleep of a labouring man is sweet, whether he eat little or much: but the abundance of the rich will not suffer him to sleep."* If you will learn to work harder, then you will find a better rest at night.

5. Working contributes to mental stability.

We live in days when mental instability seems to be all around us. Though there are several contributing factors to this, I believe one of them is that people are not working. When you don't work, you will not be satisfied with yourself.

God says, *"Commit thy works unto the Lord, and thy thoughts shall be established."* (Proverbs 16:3) Notice how working establishes your thoughts. Working has a way of making the mind a fertile field of ideas. Working keeps the mind busy, and when the mind is busy it gives stability.

6. Working gives a better retirement.

In Proverbs 6:6, the sluggard was commanded to go and watch the ant work. The ant works hard in the summer so they have something to live on in the winter. You will have a hard time building a good retirement plan if you don't work. Working gives you the ability to invest. A secure investment portfolio will not be built on poor work habits, but they will be built because you make the effort to work hard and save your money so you have something when the winter of life comes your way.

7. Working helps finance the work of the LORD.

One of the greatest reasons you need to develop a good work ethic is to be able to help the work of the LORD. 2 Corinthians 9:7 says, *"Every man according as he purposeth in his heart, so let him give; not grudgingly, or of necessity: for God loveth a cheerful giver."* You won't have anything to give to the LORD's work if you don't work. You need to understand that when you give to the LORD's work, you are giving to see souls saved. If there is ever a reason to develop a good work ethic, it is so you can invest in eternity.

These motivating factors help in developing a good work ethic. I was fortunate enough to have parents who taught me a good work ethic when I was a child. There were several things I learned from them and others that helped me in developing a work ethic that is beneficial to me and one that is scriptural. There are five basic principles to remember in developing a good work ethic.

1. Ask God to bless your work.

God says in Proverbs 16:3, *"Commit thy works unto the Lord..."* Before you start any project, you need to ask God to help your work to be productive. Working is more than just showing up for eight hours a day. Working is producing and finishing projects. You should never go a day without finishing a project. God can give you the wisdom to finish projects if you ask for His help. God wants to help you, but He will not force Himself upon you. The best habit to get into before you start anything is to ask God to bless your work by giving you the energy to work hard and the wisdom to do it right.

2. Work before you play.

One of the most important principles every person needs to learn in life is that work always comes before play. When I was a boy, my parents had chores for me to do. The rule in our house was that our chores had to be done before we could play. If we got the chores done quickly, then that gave us more time to play. This was a great motivating factor my parents used in teaching us a scriptural work ethic.

2 Thessalonians 3:10 says, *"For even when we were with you, this we commanded you, that if any would not work, neither should he eat."* God's principle is that you work before you eat. Eating is not a right but a privilege. Too many people want the

privileges without doing the work, but privileges come because of work. When looking at those who overcome average, many oftentimes covet the privileges they've acquired through hard work. If you want what they have, then work hard. It is never right to play before you work. Work comes first, then privileges can be enjoyed.

3. Be a hard worker.

The hardest working people in the world ought to be God's people. Colossians 3:23 says, *"And whatsoever ye do, do it heartily, as to the Lord, and not unto men;"* You should be known as the hardest worker at your place of employment. You'll be amazed how quickly you will rise in position if you will become the hardest worker. Hard workers will never lack a job because their work ethic will follow them and give them job security.

4. Never stand around.

My dad taught me as a young boy to never stand around on the job. He used to say, "If there is nothing else to do, then pick up a broom and sweep the floor." You are not being paid to stand around and talk, you are being paid to work. Let me take this one step further. You are not being paid to witness on the job, you are being paid to work. If you're concerned with someone's soul, then work while you are being paid to work and witness after you are off the clock. Never be caught standing around. There is always something you can do. If there is nothing to do, then find the broom and sweep the floor.

5. Make job seeking a job.

If you are without a job, then make that your job. Some make the mistake of sitting at home waiting for an employment opportunity. Instead of doing this, spend eight hours a day looking for a job and you will find it easier to get a job.

Friend, your work ethic will highly dictate whether you overcome average. If you want to be a good Christian, then develop a good work ethic. The secret to overcoming average is how hard you work. If you will work harder and longer than everyone else, and get God's wisdom to help you as you work, you will find that your work ethic will help you to rise above the average.

23

Rising Above the Average

God is not an average God. There are many gods in this world, but there is one God Who is greater than all gods, and that is Jehovah God. The psalmist said about God, *"But our God is in the heavens: he hath done whatsoever he hath pleased."* (Psalm 115:3) We can be thankful that we don't serve just an average God. The psalmist continued by comparing our God to the gods of the Earth by showing that other gods have eyes that cannot see, ears that cannot hear and mouths that cannot speak.

Our God has proven that He is not average by His works. He created a world that was not average. He created human life which is not average. He provides a salvation that is not average. When you look at the works of God it is clear to see that His works are not average because He is not an average God.

Because God is not average, you should do everything in your power to not settle for average. God does not want His children to be average; instead, He wants them to overcome average. He says in Romans 8:37, *"Nay, in all these things we are more than conquerors through him that loved us."* God didn't just want us to be conquerors; He wants us to be *"more than conquerors."* Being *"more than conquerors"* is God's challenge to every Christian to not settle for the average, but to rise above it.

When studying the Book of Proverbs, there are two people who are discussed several times. The first person is the *"sluggard."* When studying the sluggard, you see that he is an underachiever. He is lazy and idle, one who indulges in ease. The sluggard is one who wastes his potential and never strives to rise above the average because it is too hard.

The second person you will find in the Book of Proverbs is the *"diligent."* The diligent man is one who is industrious, never idle and always exerting himself to accomplish what is undertaken. He is not interested in being like everyone else, he is interested in being everything that God wants Him to be. In order to do so, he must rise above the average.

One may ask, "What is average?" Average is being typical. It is going to the standard and not doing anything more. It doing what is expected of you and nothing more. Being average is simply being like everyone else. It is the person who does what they do because everyone else does it. It is the person who only does just what is required of them and nothing more. Being average is simply giving little effort to life.

You have a choice in life to live above the line or below the line. In all reality, you are either overcoming average or you are living below average. Average is the line. You are either living above the line or below the line. God doesn't want his children to live below the line. He wants us to live above that line.

Several Scriptures show us that God wants us to do more than average. In Matthew 5, God commands the Christian to go the second mile. He says when one smites you on the right cheek, you are to turn the cheek so that you can be smitten again. God says when someone takes you to court and sues you for your coat, He says that you are not only to give your coat but also the shirt off your back. He says, *"And whosoever shall compel thee to go a mile, go with him twain."* (Matthew 5:41) God certainly shows us that He does not want us to be average.

I think of the parable of the talents in Matthew 25. There were three men who were each given a portion of talents. The one man was given five talents, and he invested those talents and came back with ten talents. Another man was given two talents. Instead of being satisfied with two talents, he was diligent to go invest them and came back with a total of four talents. The last man was given one talent. There was probably a reason he was given one talent. The man with one talent took it and dug a hole in the ground to hide the talent until his master returned. That servant was rebuked and cast away from being a servant because he did nothing to increase what was given him.

The man with one talent is very much like the average. He was satisfied with what he had. He had no initiative or drive to do more than the average. That attitude turned against him and caused him to lose everything he had. On the other hand, the other two men risked everything, and worked hard to double their return. They truly overcame average.

God wants you to rise above the average. He wants you to take whatever you have and do more with it. You can be like the man with one talent and just be average, or you can determine to exert yourself and risk all that you have to overcome average.

Overcoming average won't be easy. What you become is your choice. If you choose to be average, then you can just keep doing what you have always done. It doesn't take much effort to be average. If you choose to overcome average, you are going to have to risk everything you have. You will be criticized and attacked for your carelessness, when in reality your so called carelessness is a drive to overcome average. If you choose to overcome average, you will have to get up early and work late. You will have to sacrifice certain pleasures to overcome average. It is not that those pleasures are bad, but they will keep you from overcoming average. If you choose to overcome average, you will often be misunderstood by those who are average. They will look at you and say that you are too extreme never realizing that you are busy overcoming average.

If you choose to rise above the average, let me encourage you that you will not be in this endeavor alone. 2 Chronicles 16:9 says, *"For the eyes of the Lord run to and fro throughout the whole earth, to shew himself strong in the behalf of them whose heart is perfect toward him..."* God is looking to help the one who is willing to attempt to overcome average. God sees the one who is average and yawns, but when He sees the one who is willing to prove that God can help them rise above the average He jumps to assist them so He can show His power to this world.

Christian, you have it inside of you to overcome average. God says, *"Ye are of God, little children, and have overcome them: because greater is he that is in you, than he that is in the world."* (1 John 4:4) The question is not if you have it in you to rise above the average, because the verse above shows us that we have that power inside of us by yielding to the Holy Spirit of God.

The question comes to this, are you willing to attempt to rise above the average? Are you willing to take the risk and rise above where everyone else lives? Your rising above the average is not dependent on God; rather, it is dependent upon you doing what it takes to rise above the average. You can use every excuse in the book and be average, or you can immediately make the choice to do what it takes to rise above the average.

Friend, you will never be known for being average. People are only known for underachieving or overachieving. You never hear about anyone who is average. That is why they are average. They simply blend in with the crowd. You often hear about those who underachieved in life and the waste of the talents given to them; however, you more often hear about those who overcame average. It is the stories of those who overcame average that are used to motivate others to do great works.

The one thing that is very evident about those who strive to rise above the average is their desire. More than a desire to rise above the average, they have a hatred of being average. Their desire not to be average is what drives them to rise above the average.

The choice is clear. You can be a sluggard and simply be an underachiever who only strives for the average, or you can be the diligent person who strives to rise above the average. There will be things you must overcome, but you have a God Who is present with you to help you overcome every obstacle that tries to hold you down to average.

24

MORE TO CONQUER

In 1996 I graduated from high school. My anticipation of walking across that platform and receiving a diploma was great. Though I knew that college was next, somehow I had this thought that I would no longer have to write papers, study at night for tests or worry about getting outside assignments done.

My anticipation was to move on to the next phase of life and conquer greater heights. I couldn't wait to see what life had for me. I anticipated starting my journey of fulfilling my dreams of life, liberty, the pursuit of happiness and pleasing God. I truly had a great desire not to be average, but to do great things for God.

Little did I realize the night I walked across the platform and received my diploma that those with whom I celebrated that special night would no longer be a part of my everyday life. Somehow in our minds, we had this idea that we all would be around each other for the rest of our lives. We never thought that we would all go our separate ways and pursue what each of us had in our hearts. When I walked out of the auditorium that night, I began a journey of conquering goals, and those with whom I had spent several years in high school would no longer be a part of my journey. That journey had to be taken alone, and only what was in my heart would determine whether or not I would overcome average.

The children of Israel faced a similar choice after Joshua went to Heaven. For four hundred years Israel had overcome average. They were not like any other nation that had succumbed to Egypt's mighty hand. What others could not overcome, Israel did.

They overcame average by not allowing obstacles to stop them in their quest to the Promised Land. They overcame the whip of the Egyptian taskmaster. They overcame the unreasonable requirements of Pharaoh. They overcame the ten plagues by submitting to God's commands. They overcame the firstborn dying by applying the blood upon their doorpost. They overcame average by not letting the bondage of Egypt to stop them in their quest to get to the land God promised to them.

They overcame average by not allowing the wilderness to hold them back from the Promised Land. They overcame the negativity of the ten spies. They overcame the barren wilderness by eating manna every morning and drinking water from a rock. They overcame the Red Sea and the pursuing Egyptian army by walking through the middle of the sea. They overcame the worldly Israelites who set up a golden calf to worship. They overcame forty long years of wandering through the barren wilderness that would have caused the average to quit.

They overcame average by not allowing the giants, walls and iron chariots to prevent them from obtaining God's promise for their lives. They overcame the overflowing banks of the Jordan River. They overcame the huge walls of Jericho. They overcame armies that were greater than they. They overcame the backslidden Balaam who lured them into mingling with the enemy. They overcame every obstacle that the land of Canaan threw their way.

They experienced forty-five years of conquering, when a new generation took over. It says in Joshua 17:13, *"Yet it came to pass, when the children of Israel were waxen strong, that they put the Canaanites to tribute; but did not utterly drive them out."* This new generation had the same choice that the previous generations faced, yet this new generation settled for average. They forgot that they still had more to conquer. They looked at what they had done instead of looking at what they still had to do, and they settled for average. Instead of overcoming average and realizing they had more to conquer, they decided they would take it easy and stop conquering.

What was the result of not choosing to go forward and conquer? The result was the very people they thought they could control became their masters. Instead of learning the example of conquering from the previous generations, they settled back and chose to become average. The act of stepping back caused them to miss the enjoyment of the Promised Land that God had for them.

You face the same choice right now. You have come to the last chapter and seen what the Scriptures teach about overcoming average. What you do with what you have learned will eternally affect you, your family and those whom you influence. This is not a time to be complacent, but this is a time to reach deep inside of you and take everything you have learned and use it to help you overcome average and achieve victories for the rest of your life. No matter what your age or past accomplishments, you have more to conquer. If you are going to continue conquering, then there are five things you must do.

1. Start every day conquering.

Every day you need to conquer something. You will never overcome average without conquering. All it takes is one day not to conquer something to set up the habit of never conquering. If you never allow one day to pass without conquering something, then you will never have a second day when you don't conquer something.

Several years ago I determined that I would conquer something every day. I found that I needed to start my day off with a conquering mindset. I accomplished this by writing a devotional every day. Before I walk out the door of my house or hotel room, I have already set my mindset to conquer by finishing a devotional.

You need to have something every morning that helps you to set a mindset to conquer. Start your day out conquering by making your bed, reading the Scriptures and spending a few minutes in prayer. Then, walk out your door and determine that you will not lay your head on your pillow that night without having something else that you have conquered throughout the day.

2. Don't settle for the average.

Those who have a conquering mindset will not settle for average. Determine that you are not going to live your life like everyone else. Find God's will for your life and make the most of it. Don't just settle with doing average, but get something inside you that drives you to do more than others. Dream big, work hard, and never stop pursuing God's dreams for your life.

3. Don't listen to the negative.

When you determine to overcome average, you are going to have to get ready to hear negative people tell you that you can't do it. Friend, if you are saved, you have a God who can help you overcome average. Plug your ears to the naysayers and listen by faith to a God who calls you to be *"more than conquerors."*

Separate yourself from the negative and surround yourself with people who push you to get the most out of yourself. Don't look to surround yourself with people who allow you to easily get by with average; rather, surround yourself with people who motivate you to do more than you thought you could ever do. Surround yourself with people who are positive and believe that God can enable all of us to do great things for Him.

4. Remember your future.

Sin always stops you from conquering. Always remember that every action will impact your future. Before you choose to do anything, remember there will be consequences to those actions. Don't ruin your future for one night of pleasure. Always remember that in everything you do there will be a payday tomorrow. Don't sacrifice your future for the immediate. Those who overcome average always remember there are consequences tomorrow for today's actions. They realize that today's decisions determine tomorrow's destiny.

5. Keep God in every aspect of your life.

You will never overcome average without God. This book is not a self-help book, it is not a self-improvement book, but it is a God-help book. One of the main purposes of this book is to remind you that with God included in every aspect of your life, you can overcome average. God says in Matthew 6:33, *"But seek ye first the kingdom of God, and his righteousness; and all these things shall be added unto you."* God wants to help you overcome average, but you will never do it without putting Him first in everything you do in life. God is the only One Who can help you overcome average, and that is why He must be first in all of your priorities of life.

Friend, let these last few words be the end of an average life. Live your life with a determination that you will overcome average. Don't let the greatest and most productive years of your life be in the past. I challenge you to make this the first step of overcoming average. If your life is going to be one of overcoming average, then from this moment forward you must serve God, dream big, work hard, do your best and don't quit.